Andreas Dvořák

Humanity 10.0

Shaping our future together!

Andreas Dvořák

Humanity 10.0

Shaping our
future together!

Preface and acknowledgements

How many stages of development has humanity been through?
How many concepts for the development of our societies already exist?

When will we humans become a true world community?
I have not found the answers to these questions.
Therefore »Humanity 10.0« evolved as a proposal for the further development of humanity towards a randomly chosen level / version 10.0.

This is a book about a future worth living for all people. It is based on us as humans and our ability to ultimately make the right decisions.

Humanity has reached a crossroads. We will only survive if we are able to positively shape the future with common visions and concrete plans.

»Humanity 10.0« is a building block for the future that can help us meet upcoming challenges.

True to the concept of working together to shape the future, several people have already provided helpful feedback on »Humanity 10.0« or collaborated on it.

I would like to thank my family and friends for their cooperation and understanding. Developing the ideas as well as working on the book was time-consuming, time which was almost certainly lacking elsewhere.

My sincere gratitude to everyone who has had a special part. Many thanks to Andrea, Aline, Alexander, Carmen, Heike and Ralf, Karin and Gert, Barbara and Andreas, as well as Jolanta and Edwin, who also translated the book into English and French.

In the hope that the effort was worthwhile - enjoy reading the book!

Table of contents

Five questions and the book

The five questions that are so important for us, are easily formulated.
Is everything that is currently around us and
what should/could/will happen in future, positive or negative for:

- The individual **human** (you / me)?
- My/our **surroundings**?
- My/our **community**?
- The entire **environment**?
- **Humanity** as a whole?

The questions arise as common areas of focus for people, regardless of the form of society in which they live. The book provides many ideas and links, however, the most interesting is that based on these five questions, a concept for a better future can be developed.

Most people are interested in the present and the near future and they also remember the past. Thinking about visions, goals, and our future often needs impulses at first. This is the intention of the section "At the Beginning".

Facts from our environment follow in Part 1, "What surrounds us". The intention of these is to further introduce the topic and underline the necessity of »Humanity 10.0«. Trends are particularly important. These play a significant role in determining what our future will look like. A future concept can influence trends early on and sustainably for the benefit of people, so that corrections that cannot be avoided become necessary later.

Part 2, »Humanity 10.0«, describes the idea, the approach, and the principles of »Humanity 10.0«. In addition to the visions, goals and principles are defined, which seem particularly important for »Humanity 10.0« and for the development of adaptable societies. In order to achieve the goals and to be able to manage the complexity of a future concept, the development of a simple, universal, and future-proof values / rating system is proposed. This can develop in parallel to everything that already exists. The basic ideas behind this are described but it is up to us humans to develop it in detail. This will require a lot of scientific creativity and a great deal of expertise.

Part 3, "How does »Humanity 10.0« operate?" takes up individual topics from Part 1 "What surrounds us". It explains how »Humanity 10.0« should be applied and which impacts can be achieved.
The focus of this part is to increase understanding and encourage reflection on the further potential of the concept.

One of the most pressing questions is: How can »Humanity 10.0« be introduced? A plan for the introduction is available in Part 4, "Introducing »Humanity 10.0« ".
As it is not possible to estimate how quickly the ideas will spread, no statement can be made regarding the time frames. If, as intended, an increase in all social forces follows, the efficiency and pace of introduction will increase.
As far as the implementation of ideas and enforcement of change is concerned, many tools and extensive know-how already exist.

Part 5, "Motivation" is intended to further stimulate the desire to think about the future. Here, additional aspects are presented, which illustrate how thinking about the future in the context of »Humanity 10.0« can lead to new ideas.
Furthermore, this part includes the presentation of benefits for various organisations and for us humans.

Part 6, "Finally" includes a summary, remarks, and an outlook.

The appendix includes the "Detailed description of the values/ rating system", as well as notes on the procedure for the rating of issues.

At the beginning

Introduction

Since the beginning of humanity, the opinions about what we humans can influence have always differed. What can we or cannot we change?

What we consider to be able to effectively influence, is very much dependant on our personal perceptions and character traits.

"Where there is one body, there cannot be another." This is a simple and recognised concept in physics.

A person can exert influence, for example, by moving a car. If the car is moved to a place where another car is already located, a collision will occur. We understand this and accept it.

There could be other factors playing a role in connection with the accident and collision, such as slippery roads, bad tires, and malfunctioning brakes. We can recognise these factors and take them into account in future.

The driver is not only injured – he dies. What was responsible for his death? Why exactly did this person have to die?

In life, many questions remain unanswered.

When questions remain unanswered, we fill that void with new knowledge, speculations, distraction, hope…or we are at a loss for answers and helpless.

There will always be unanswered questions.

However, there are issues, on which we humans have direct or indirect influence. This book focusses on these issues and knowledge-based information.

The predominantly philosophical aspects relating to the meaning of us as humans and our actual influence do not play a major role.

We humans have been around for approximately two million years and, up to now, we have always adapted or had to adapt to various living conditions.

The right combination of taking short-term action and making long-term change in our behaviour patterns was the key to success.

Nowadays not completely unfounded doubts exist about the (too) short-term actions taken by us humans and goal-oriented strategies for mastering current and future challenges are lacking.
Some people fear this situation, others have ceased thinking about the complexity of the world or do not see a chance to initiate the changes that are necessary.

Currently attempts are being made to compensate for the lack of suitable strategies through increasingly short-term activities. This is not very helpful, because it leads to unrest and insecurity amongst us humans and deprives many of the hope for a future worth living.

But there is also another side; people who are enthusiastically committed to the well-being of all and are optimistic about the future.
The current focus is often on improving individual living conditions. In the case of medium- and long-term issues, the focus is on environmental and climate protection.

»Humanity 10.0« aims to convey a vision and provide hope and optimism through a concept for the development of sustainable societies, as well as paving the way towards a future with more satisfaction.

»Humanity 10.0« is based on facts, however the importance of ethical values and differences in perception are, in no way ignored. "Humans" are the focus, but not every subjective perception of reality can be considered.

The best way to deal with reality is to accept it openly and objectively. This includes seeing ourselves as part of the bigger picture and recognising our strengths and weaknesses. Our future depends on the ability to work together and protect our environment.

By incorporating the aspects presented in »Humanity 10.0«, the chances are good that we will be able to rise to the challenges facing us.

»Humanity 10.0« is targeted at everyone.

At families, who are concerned about their children's future.

At leading organisations and personalities, who must, or rather should, ensure the future of all people.

Progressive organisations and visionaries should be given a platform, in order to be able to combine forces.

»Humanity 10.0« is intended to give hope to the disillusioned and discouraged, as well as the possibility to reorient.

»Humanity 10.0« offers every single person and each organisation chances to further develop.

This book is not a novel, not prose, not a thriller, not an operating instruction manual and not a scientific paper, it is a combination of many things. It somehow combines all the above; also dreams, the possible "happy end" and the suspense of whether it can succeed. Behind many seemingly trivial thoughts, there is a deeper meaning waiting to be discovered.

Ultimately, the book aims to encourage first "intellectual self-attempts" at rating current issues and trends.

Thinking about what the future holds for us all is not something that we do every day, which is why the first chapters of this book are intended as a warming-up phase.

Wake up!

A survey under the heading "Was it better in the old days?" carried out by television channels in about 60 countries, came up with the interesting results.

All survey results are available and can be sorted by various criteria.

The survey was designed for young people, but open to whoever wanted to participate.

There were varying percentages in the different age groups, however the general trend of responses was predominantly the same.

Despite country-specific variations, definite trends showed up in the responses.

Even if the participants did not represent the average of the population groups, 300,000 opinions cannot be so easily ignored.

The future is seen in a more negative light by all (regardless of age) compared to the past or present.
This is concerning and rather sad.

Two thirds of the respondents stated that, "it is true – the generations of our parents and grandparents are responsible for the difficulties of young people today".

Many parts of the survey showed that action must be taken at long last and that new ideas are needed.

The survey results must make us all sit up and think.

This remarkable survey can be accessed under:
https://www.time-to-question.com/en/results

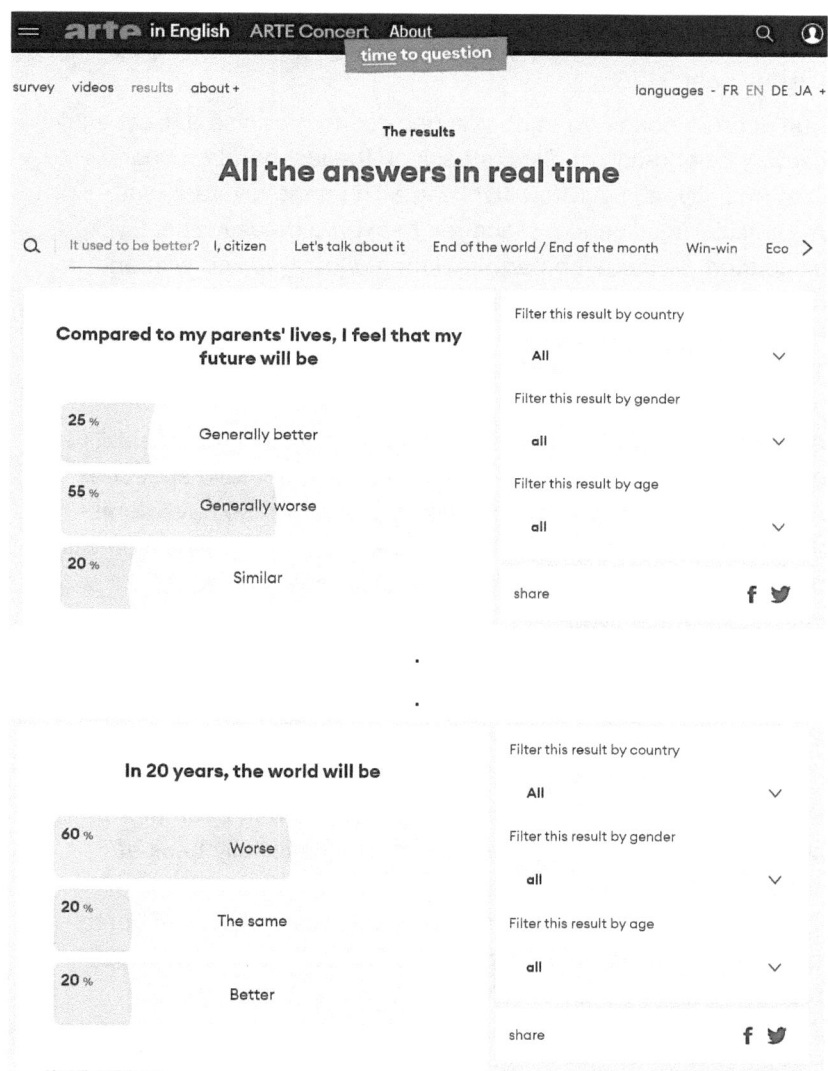

Figure 1: ARTE 2020 Survey

2120

It is the year 2120.

The supreme body on earth has decided to organise a great anniversary celebration and looks back on the last hundred years. Just recently, a joint effort involving all humans, avatars, and AI (artificial intelligence) managed to avert a catastrophe. Ever since then, all those on earth feel more closely linked with one another, or at least they accept the fact that they only have a future if they join forces.

This tolerant feeling of belonging together is partly the result of painful experiences.

At the anniversary celebration, the most important representatives of the humans, as well as the avatars and AI will hold speeches. All other living beings on earth would probably also have something to say, however, even in the year 2120, communication with animals. plants or less complex creatures has not yet been successfully achieved.

People's hope that genetic decoding would make it easier to understand why relatively simple creatures survive for millennia and that complex humans are comparatively vulnerable, has proven to be a fallacy.

With the realisation that apart from genes, further, even more complex interrelationships exist, science is basically back at square one.

This discovery and various failures in the manipulation of hereditary material, have at least led to the fact that people stopped producing clones of themselves.

Thus, the focus moved towards the development of avatars. As a combination of AI and human components, these should really be called "cyborgs" (cybernetics organism). Avatars were originally graphic computer figures. The sympathetic portrayal of these human-like beings in the successful 3D film "Avatar" increased their popularity, as well as their significance.

Because the production of individual organs is no longer a major challenge in 2120, the resemblance of avatars to human beings is very high. However, the integrated, complex, and understandable logic of AI determines their actions.

Experiments carried out in order to provide avatars with feelings failed because feelings are difficult to comprehend and sometimes lead to erratic and uncontrollable behaviour. Apart from that, the inclusion of feelings would result in too many different avatars and make production too complex.

Avatars, half human, and half AI, are an important group on earth, endowed with rights and duties.

KI apparatuses and supercomputers manufactured from semicon-ductors had nothing human about them, thus humans did not ini-tially grant AI any human-like rights. In addition, the centralised learning of AI on supercomputers proved to consume far too much energy, thus limiting the application options.

Decentralised AI, however, resulted in significant progress being made. Thus, individual robots equipped with more and more intelligence were able to act independently.

With the production of individual parts of AI from biological material and the assumption of important functions in the human body, AI also received an appropriate status on earth.

Representatives of humans, avatars and AI are pondering on what could be included in their speeches at the anniversary celebration. Usually anniversaries include jubilant recollections of success stories. This would, however not correspond with the reality in this case and objectivity is one of the most important common rules in 2120.

It was possible to avert the last catastrophe, despite the many differences of opinion in the run-up. The situation was clear, a super volcano was about to erupt. As a result of this rather local event, the earth would have darkened for several years.

Besides enormous problems keeping humans supplied with the basics, some animal and plant species would even have died out.

People very nearly returned to their old ways of thinking, as a result of the approaching "super volcano eruption" catastrophe. A part of the people felt less affected because the volcano was very far away. In some regions, people would have welcomed the cooling effect of the resulting darkening effect. On the other hand, others wanted to counter the cooling in their region with the resulting warming up of the earth. Other solutions to the problem, such as clearing the atmosphere of dust over a large area with "flying vacuum cleaners" after the eruption, were not any more intelligent. Actually, the volcanic eruption and its aftermath did not affect AI and the robots. In fact, they could have rid themselves of the annoying humans and their power if it had not been for the new-fangled agreement to help each other solve problems. Thus "AI" carefully calculated everything and came up with the conclusive decision.

Speaking of which, there was really no such thing as "the AI". The nation states had recognized the importance of AI, especially the super computers. These super computers, were well-shielded by the nation-states and provided with logics designed to ensure power and dominance. In special cases "national AIs" worked together. What about the big AI corporations?
As these became too powerful and began to put their profit interests above the welfare of humans, they were crushed. Thus, they were only able to deal with decentralised AI.

What could be the solution for the super volcano eruption now?

In a way, the pressure had to be released from the earth. For this purpose, an exact copy of the earth's crust was created, including all the magma chambers and exit points of gases and magma. Pressures were measured, material samples taken and ultimately, it was possible to determine where and how best to allow gases and magma to escape, without causing a catastrophe.

Humans were, of course, unsuitable for the work required and avatars were too vulnerable. Thus, AI had thousands of its combat robots converted, which then sacrificed themselves for the benefit of the humans.

There was no shortage of combat robots. The nation states had produced them in large numbers until they realised that this was a pointless arms race. Humans therefore actually wanted to put an end to the arms race. At this point, however, robots were able to develop and produce other robots. AI was no longer dependent on new knowledge coming from humans.

The time felt right to take control of the "illogical" humans. Even more combat robots were developed by AI and produced by other combat robots. The fate of humanity seemed to be sealed.

But what saved the humans?

As the combat robots came into the focus of the public eye, the nation states agreed that that every robot should be equipped with an "emergency stop button". However, since this is a strategic disadvantage in the case of war, not a single state complied.

Anyway, in many cases, contractual agreements were only in place to pacify the respective populations.

Humans spent centuries developing and building things for their own destruction and by no means always kept to agreements.

For AI it was absolutely clear that this situation would not change in future, which is why AI took over most of the functions of the combat robots developed by humans, without controlling each one. In the meantime, the functions of the robots had become so complex that only a few humans and robots could maintain an overview. In the end, humanity owes its survival to a small group of developers; these had not deactivated the "emergency stop button", as demanded by their governments, but had kept to the actual contractual regulations.

Thus, the still active "emergency stop button" was involuntarily integrated into all other combat robots. In this way, the combat robots could be made capable of action at the decisive moment and humanity could be saved.

Fortunately, there are always people who will take huge risks for granted, in order to put the well-being of the community before their own.

Perhaps that is why AI got so involved in the imminent super volcanic eruption because it had a "bad conscience", or rather the humans owed it something. Because intelligent logic also requires that the relation of give and take must be balanced.

When it comes down to it, it is important that the right thing happens and not why it happens.
It is far better to invest energy and resources in the present and future, rather than dwelling on the past.
Establishment of guilt should pave the way for being able to make amends. Something that is good should continue to be something good.
This sounds like plausible logic – or not?

It may sound crazy, but it was only after humans trained AI to be intelligent, did they themselves become intelligent.
AI always pursues neutral, reality-oriented clear logics and humans …well.
A kind of competition arose between AI and humans. The more intelligent AI became, the more humans realised, how ridiculously their actions sometimes were. AI indirectly uncovered their faulty actions for the humans.
This may be the reason why humans are more drawn towards avatars as to AI.

The pleasant avatars, who are like humans, are, in the meantime, all over the earth. They serve humans and take on the more unpleasant tasks and responsibilities.
Even though avatars are free of emotions, many humans are close to them and regard them as friends.
Most avatars are not assigned to just one person but rather to a community. Many tasks are solely carried out by avatars.
Avatars are produced in a decentralised manner, they are, however closely linked to one another by their uniform characteristics and communication. This almost blind understanding is immensely useful.

Wars and other ways of pursuing power have been a major problem for humanity in past decades. The "superpowers" did not comprehend that greatness does not result from power, but from working towards the well-being of people.
Thus, the "superpowers" continually attempted to maintain their supremacy and other states strived to attain the same status. They were even prepared to wage wars, as well as to accept the risks of mass destruction weapons.
People were persuaded that peace could only be secured through deterrence, or even by staging wars. Thus, people were not only manipulated, but nationalism and hatred were also stirred up. Unfortunately, many people did not care, if it did not affect them; others felt somehow helpless.

The avatars played a key role in this situation.
The programming of the avatars is focussed on the well-being of people and the community. Wars and other conflicts pose a threat to people, avatars, and AI.
When warlike conflicts were in the pipeline, the avatars world-wide came to an agreement very quickly and finally put an end to the pointless striving for power.
The avatars of the warmongers and the human rights violators, not only failed to serve their owners, but also ensured they receive a just punishment.
For a short time, the avatars took complete control and thus created a true world community. In this way, the truly important values could be established worldwide.

Would people have been able to come to an all-out agreement in such a short space of time?
People were speechless as to how quickly and sustainably problems can be solved through unity.
Have people fundamentally changed in one hundred years?
No – but there are always solutions to go about dealing with weaknesses in an intelligent manner.
Those who fulfil their responsibility to society and meet the needs

of the community can live out their "weaknesses" without social consequences, like envy. The basic conditions, however, are not to harm anyone by one's own actions, to take full responsibility for them and to bear the consequences oneself.

For example, in the year 2042, the existing car racing tracks were opened for "speeders", where they can pursue their hobby there using environmentally-friendly vehicles.
As far as the community was concerned, this had many positive results. Traffic flow could be better optimised, without the disruption caused by speeding. The number of traffic accidents decreased. All other road users simply felt better on the roads.

Does 2120 suddenly represent the "ideal world"? No, it does not. On the one hand, too many consequences of the past still exist. The temperatures on earth are still too high. The fight to stop climate change was started too late and was not conducted consistently enough. Plastic and other litter continued to pollute the oceans. Industrial plant production and animal husbandry, as well as the extensive production of chemicals, led to the contamination of even the last remaining resources. As water works its way through soil very slowly,
it will take decades before groundwater is clean again.
On the other hand, several threats exist for which humanity does not yet have adequate backup plans. For some, short-term decisions continue to be more important than long-term strategies.

There are however, several success stories to look back on in the year 2120. Alternative energy production was able to meet almost all the needs of the entire planet. Recycling is no longer just a façade; mountains of waste are the new resources. It is not all good. The crucial thing is however, that people have changed their way of thinking and are focussing on essentials.

For an anniversary celebration, it is just as important to look back enthusiastically at what has been achieved, as to what is on the list of tasks still to be mastered. An anniversary should be an opportunity to look back to the beginning and take stock. Even in the year 2120, historians did not entirely agree, whether the occasion for the celebrations goes back to 2020 or 2021.

Both years saw the peak of the worldwide coronavirus pandemic. This served to open people's eyes somewhat. People saw that they were far from being in control. For crises such as these, there was both a lack of sound contingency plans, such as concrete precautionary measures. For example, there were too few protective masks, respirators, intensive care beds and vaccines.
Many people hoped that the coronavirus pandemic would have all sorts of positive effects. Others wanted to get back to normality as soon as possible – that is, not change anything. The acceptance of the measures taken, depended, in many ways, from everyone's personal attitude. It could never be clarified which role the coronavirus pandemic played in the important changes.
A very favourable effect was, however, demonstrable. When another pandemic occurred 35 years later, whereby a death rate of 25% occurred, emergency plans were in place and everyone knew what was essential.

It is important to mention the idea which was initiated in the year 2020, to stop climate change by mass-planting trees. However, in that very year, the great drought triggered by climate change in many areas, led to trees dying on an unprecedented scale.
In addition to that was the increase in slash-and-burn agriculture. Even if the responsibility for this lay with individual governments and even individuals, the real causes were greed for profit, nationalistic egoism, and short-term thinking.
For example, the head of the government of the country with the most slash-and-burn operations ignored any climate concerns. But that person was not the only one who acted this way. In 2020 people in many countries failed to elect suitable governments to serve their people. Why not?

Populism and fake news prevented people from getting on track and being able to make realistic ratings of the situation.
Governments and large corporations even blocked important

information and necessary developments, in the interest of maintaining their own power.

Other organizations subordinated themselves to the power structure. Thus, in many countries there was a web of greed for money and power, corruption, and private gain.

Non-governmental and non-profit initiatives had not had sufficient supporters and influence yet. They also did not join forces often enough.

The trend changed in the years 2020/2021. The unnecessary populism and distortion of the truth were pushed back. This certainly had something to do with the fact that the biggest populist of them all had lost the election in his country. He now served as a cautionary example and progressive forces were able to develop better again. Some of his imitators remained in power, but the turnaround had been accomplished. But was this turnaround so significant that it could still be celebrated a hundred years later?

Another important event occurred less than one hundred years ago This was particularly crucial for the avatars and robots. Solar storms are a well-known ever re-occurring phenomenon. When these happen, the sun hurls large quantities of material into the universe and in the direction of earth. The electric and magnetic fields protect the earth from normal amounts of matter and energy. However, sometimes giant solar storms occur. Their enormous energy reaches the earth's surface and destroys, mainly electrical and electronic components and systems, for example those that ensure the supply of power and functioning communication. Any kind of electronic application is at risk. Because people were dependent on the ever-available electrical power and electronic communication, even minor setbacks led to everything breaking down and general panic. Widespread power cuts and communication breakdown due to a solar storm has catastrophic consequences, even if there is no immediate risk for the lives of living beings on earth.

As the likelihood of an extreme solar storm increased, people took protective measures. Important electrical and electronic components and equipment were designed to be better protected against cosmic rays. Central AI and major computing and communications centres were sheltered in caves and other safe places with their own power supplies.

In 2058, a devastating solar storm occurred. Many robots and avatars were moved to safety. However, particularly older, electrical, and electronic components and systems, as well as robots and avatars lacked any protection. Thus, the solar storm not only caused considerable damage, but mass destruction occurred among the older robots and avatars.

That was the time when humans still ruled over the lawless robots and avatars. Humans demanded their services despite the imminent danger of the solar storm. The death of their robots and avatars was a punishment for the humans, since they themselves had to deal with long-forgotten tasks, with which they were totally overwhelmed. This was a decisive factor leading to robots and avatars being granted first real rights, as had already been talked about long before. They became a part of the vast community on earth.

A further small episode in connection with the solar storm is also interesting. Due to a fortunate circumstance, humans were only indirectly affected by the solar storm.

Most people like to arrange their lives as comfortably as possible and this with little opposition. Those not wanting to participate because they fear negative consequences are outvoted. Thus by 2040 almost all people had had an identification chip implanted. They were, for instance, able to shop without being delayed at the checkout. ID cards were no longer necessary, checks could be passed without major delays.

However, the chip in the body was not really a good solution because instead of ID cards or cell phones being stolen, chip cards were forcibly removed, thus often causing serious injuries. People's identity was no longer their own, but the chip with the parts of the electronic image of that person. People were forced to prove their own physical identity, often at great expense. Ultimately there was a fundamental rethink.

Automatic identification continued to take place; however, it was completely converted to a combination of many optical, biological, chemical, and electrical features.

If people had still been equipped with chips in the year 2058, the solar storm would have damaged them in the same way as all electronic components and they would have lost their identity.

We have still not yet managed to discover what was behind the centenary celebration.

The fact that asteroids passed the earth, the temperatures on earth reached new records together with discoveries and inventions... – but what has shaped humanity up to the year 2120, and changed it for the better?

The initially seemingly unspectacular ideas behind »Humanity 10.0« have revolutionised the world over the following decades.

In 2020, the first Internet page of »Humanity 10.0« was created and the symbol was registered as a word-image-brand.

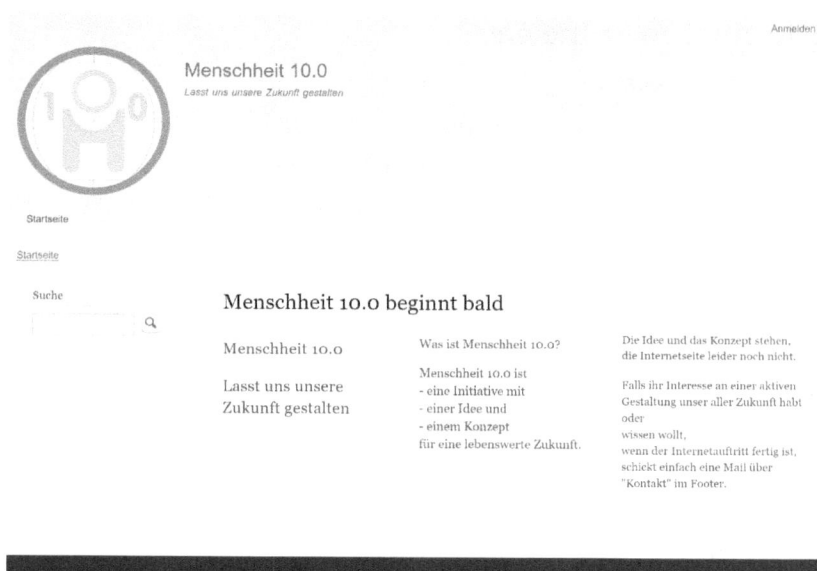

Figure 2: The first internet page of »Menschheit 10.0«

The chicken or the egg?

Which or what came first?

Which or what is more important?

What is the right approach to »Humanity 10.0«?
Is it our current situation with all the respective challenges or is it the dreams and visions of a bright future?

Many things coexist and complement each other.
Everyone has their own way of thinking and acting, their own views and preferences.
It is important to accept this and try to be objective when weighing things up – even if we are inclined to take one side.

After a neutral kick-off to the idea of »Humanity 10.0«, we focus on current issues and trends.

Ultimately however, it is interesting to see all that »Humanity 10.0« involves.

Introduction to the idea

One could continue to write the book in the style of "2120" or continue to philosophise about "the chicken and the egg"- situation. As appealing as this thought is, there would then perhaps be no year 2120 at all for us humans.

Many readers would consume the book as light reading and remember it as being a nice diversion, but it would not fulfil the actual purpose. The aim of the book is to point out a way to a bright future and to encourage reflection and, above all, action.

The future is the present of tomorrow.

Is this a foolish saying?
Or does it not depict the consequences far too clearly?

We want to live as long as possible, but we do not really know how we want to live.
Unpleasant events diminish our strength and quality of life, yet we are not sufficiently prepared to prevent them. How often do we personally devote ourselves to thinking about the future? How much do we invest in it?

It seems as if we have too little time, too much on our plates to see the necessity of thinking about the future.
Are we perhaps even afraid of the future or of the realisation that our importance in the big picture is much smaller than we would like it to be?
At the same time, the future is so strongly linked to hope.
We all like to dream and make plans for the future. These thoughts feed on hope and give impetus to our feeling of satisfaction and our strength. The focus is not on our dreams coming true. The visions dreamed about are often, too vague.
Fear of the future often arises if the future is considered passively. This impotence or indifference drains people's energy, they look for another source of stability or give up.

»Humanity 10.0« aims to stimulate thinking about the future, in order to provide hope and strength.

Fear of this reflection is not justified.

In the past, people doubted their right to exist, on other occasions they succumbed to illusions of grandeur. Ultimately people were always quite successful in finding solutions.

Currently, there are also many suitable approaches. Unfortunately, priorities are not always set correctly so that too much energy is poured into projects which are relatively unimportant for humanity.

The questions related to what our future should hold and how we as humans want to live together should be more proactive and preferably answered more objectively.

The "I'm against it" opinion helps just as little as turning certain topics or proposals into taboos. We need to understand as many interrelationships as possible and take them into account in the plan for our future.

»Humanity 10.0« focuses on current trends and issues. It looks at the significance these have on us humans, why good ideas do not always prevail and demonstrates how a change could come about. The extent of issues and possibilities is colossal.

The proposal for a new universal values/rating system is intended to make this more manageable.

A current dilemma is that in the seemingly more and more complex word mainly extremes are perceived and short-term thinking and acting dominates. This is highly problematic because extremes and a short-term perception of things are considered as being normal. Thus, it is even more difficult for sustainable topics and long-term strategies to gain acceptance.

If we humans do not develop common visions and goals, our lives will not really improve, despite all the progress made.

In the coming decades, we must decide if we want to be (remain) rational human beings or end up as vulnerable biological machines?

Catastrophes are not always foreseeable.

However, we humans should not trigger these ourselves.

For other threats, we require contingency plans to help us through the crises.

Unfortunately, we are not acting rationally and prudently at present and we are not taking sufficient precautions in the case of crises.

»Humanity 10.0« has visions and goals, but also a sustainable concept. It aims to secure our survival, further develop societies, as well as increasing people's satisfaction.

Despite the resulting complexity and large number of areas to be covered, a new model for the future can be developed by using a simple solution-oriented approach.

We cannot change the inactivity of the great ship "humanity" in the short term but we can take the right long-term course now.

Essential elements

»Humanity 10.0« aims to cover as many issues and trends as possible and to offer versatile opportunities for cooperation.

The visions and goals should be supported by most people even if the ideas and solutions differ to a certain extent.

The "uniform person" is just as undesirable as self-absorbed individuals with completely differing moral concepts.

Nation states are not necessarily a hindrance but we cannot afford to have egoistic nationalism on earth in the long run.
Democratic discussions are helpful, but must, at some stage, get to the point.
Dictatorial instructions can speed up decisions, however, they diminish flexibility and innovation.

»Humanity 10.0« is about the development of well-balanced, adaptive societies, that can react optimally to necessary changes and are oriented to the feasible wishes of us humans.

Even if it is not easy to change our ways of thinking, the power of shared visions and goals will ultimately lead to a positive sense of "we" and to plausible benefits for each individual.

The ideas behind »Humanity 10.0« can only be realised if we take our future in our own hands as a community and work together to implement new visions and goals.

All those interested, as well as those who have not yet been directly involved with the development of the future are cordially invited to read the book.

Due to the wide-ranging claim of »Humanity 10.0« and the interesting challenges regarding its implementation, everyone can contribute to shaping the future.
If you would like to actively help to shape the future or require fur-ther information, please visit the website:
www.humanity10.org

Part 1: What surrounds us

Introduction

The next sections will be dedicated to current contexts and challenges. These examples are intended to be an initial stimulus to think about topics and issues.
Future solutions can only be found based on comprehensive analyses of the current situation.
Objective ratings and criteria are indispensable and ensure the correct reference to the chosen issues.
Subjective perceptions must also not be disregarded. Albeit, these aspects, as well as accusations regarding undesirable developments in the past, do not play a role in this part.

Current trends highlight possible development tendencies. For influencing trends, »Humanity 10.0« can be of decisive importance, serving as a bond between us humans.

Some topics already include a reference to »Humanity 10.0«. The chosen order of topics is arbitrary, regardless of their significance or possible improvement potential.

Current topics

Interdependence of people and globalisation

It is obvious how interlinked societies are and how dependent we humans are on each other. There is sometimes a severe division of labour on both national and global levels. We humans are social beings and cannot survive on our own.

Globalisation is a fact. All humans on earth use oxygen, water and other resources and live on worldwide available animals and plants. Mobility knows no restrictions. Ecosystems change through global blending. Diseases know no borders. Developments are global in many areas.

What is missing in global development and transnational thinking is optimisation in the interests of all people on earth. This is the reason why many people question the sense of globalisation or sometimes reject it.

Growth

Constant or even unlimited growth cannot and will not exist in a world of exhaustible resources. This fact is not particularly difficult to understand. Yet this is exactly the principal we use to create whole societies, "limitless growth". We are incredibly frightened of carcinogenic substances, but at the same time, we accept the constant growth of our societies as a "huge tumour".

Why do we find it so difficult to change this situation?
Perhaps this is because of a weakness we human have, one that is not new - greed. Our weaknesses must be considered if long-term concepts are to be successful. At the same time, business models that are based on human weaknesses must be hindered. If there are good reasons to do so, we humans can and will change.

Environmental protection

Even without further growth, we are already using up more resources than are available in the long-run. This is nothing new,
but still hardly anything changes.

Are we victims of our own complacency and only bring about
changes when it is almost too late? Or would we like to "wash –
but not get"?
It is hopefully not a question of human arrogance towards the
complex system of nature, because that would mean our certain
downfall.

We have already caused so much damage on the earth that it will
be impossible to put everything to rights, at least in the medium term.
Environmental protection will be one of the central tasks of the
coming decades, if not centuries. We must set the right priorities
now, in order to develop and bring about sustainable changes.

Sacrifice

We humans find it difficult to do without. Sacrificing leads to negative emotions, even if brings about something that is positive, such
as improved health or an intact environment.
If something has already become part of our lives, if we have become accustomed to property or comforts, it is particularly difficult
to sacrifice them. We even find it difficult to forgo things which are
only possibly attainable, such as flights or cruises. This behaviour
can already be observed in children; it is a characteristic and
seemingly begins in the cradle.

What can we do, if sacrifice is unavoidable?
Recognise the necessity.
In doing so we would simultaneously secure our "freedom."
Is "freedom" not the realisation of necessity?
However, a concept for the future cannot be based solely on in-
sights, it must also offer intelligent solutions.
We could reduce apparent sacrifice by stopping to artificially cre-
ate needs. Many products have no actual added value for us.

We want to own them because they are cleverly anchored in our lives through advertising. If we do not get these products, we see this as a sacrifice.

If sacrifice is unavoidable, alternatives must be identified, in order to maintain or increase satisfaction. This can be achieved, for example through other values.

Time constants

"Rome wasn't built in a day", "Good things come to those who wait." These are not just sayings; the message behind them is the realisation that every development and every change require a certain amount of time. Under specific circumstances, this period can be shortened within the bounds of what is reasonable.

As positive as optimism is, it can be detrimental when estimating required time periods. Incorrectly estimating the time required for something is annoying and can certainly be improved.

However, there are serious cases of severe and deliberate disregard of temporal connections.

Everyone knows how tediously slow large organisations can be (for example companies). Business developments are subject to long periods of time and employees have limited potential to change at short-notice. Changes usually take years to happen. However, if you look at the value of a company on the stock exchange, it can change within a very short period (milliseconds in high-frequency trading).

These two-time ranges for one and the same thing, "the value of a company" do not match up. Visions, concepts, and changes especially those that are highly complex, need time. Short-term hypes are of no use for the long-term development of our future.

Populism

Most people feel more comfortable with their own opinion, rather than having to deal with other opinions or even being forced to accept them. Feeling connected with others by a consensus is a good thing and demonstrates that we humans are social beings.

Populism takes advantage of this mechanism and seemingly accepts people's wishes, to disguise and better assert its own goals. A lot of promises are made which cannot be held, or rather should not be held, for logical reasons.

The approach of »Humanity 10.0« considers people's wishes and which conditions must be met, to fulfil expectations is made transparent. »Humanity 10.0« also incorporates unpopular topics. Proposals and critical suggestions are considered as the basis for further improvements.

Falsehood and truth

"Fake News" is not an invention of modern times. The spread of falsehoods has always existed. They were often refuted by reality, unfortunately, usually when it was too late.

"Alternative facts" could be considered as being a type of freedom of opinion. Everyone can decide how to view them or what to think about them. However, "alternative facts" are mostly used to distort the truth and are nothing more than lies that do not reflect reality.

Why has it become increasingly difficult to recognise the truth? For one thing, anonymity and technical know-how relating to the internet has made it easier to spread lies.
On the other hand, the flood of information is so huge that it has become impossible to promptly refute all lies.
Unfortunately, new technological opportunities tend to be rapidly misused, mostly because of power or profit interests. Technological development has become so fast, that in many cases, necessary corrective measures come too late.
However, the issues mentioned would play a lesser role if a consensus on moral values were in place before new developments crop up.

We humans will not suddenly start telling the truth all the time. But morally dominated standards focussed on what is important to us, could reduce the number of lies considerably.

Freedom, democracy, and dictatorship

We humans will always have to deal with dependencies. The better we understand these, the less restrictive they seem to be.

Humanity has developed many forms of organisational structures for coexistence over the course of time. The currently most important are democracy and dictatorship. One can argue about which social order is better. The fact is that both, very different approaches, have pros, as well as cons.
This is of particular interest for »Humanity 10.0« because the systems are, in part, irreconcilably opposed to each other. The conflicts could even endanger the future of all people.

»Humanity 10.0« aims to help resolve confrontations. By focussing strongly on the facts, »Humanity 10.0« aims to strive for a certain independence from social organisational forms.

Increase in the world's population

Neither people's attitudes to this subject, nor the reasons for the drastic increase in the world's population are important. To date, nature has always managed to regulate drastic population growth. After a critical number had been reached, there was a reduction of the species back to a normal level. In many cases, this reduction was triggered by a shortage of resources or a reduction of habitat.

So, if we do not get a grip on the waste of our resources or habitats continue to decrease because of global warming, many humans will perish. Letting people die is profoundly inhumane. There is widespread consensus on that point.
But why are opinions sometimes so irreconcilably opposed, when it comes to determining a "reasonable" number of human beings on earth to fend off humane consequences?

Responsibility for the future of humanity

Great philosophers, scientists, and distinguished personalities have addressed humans and their coexistence. This resulted in different findings, models, and recommendations, but also in a consensus on many issues.

We humans are not all the same; we have different skills, opinions, … and therefore different roles in communities, which is why hierarchies have always had a role in our communal lives and why we will not be able to do without comparable structural orders in future.

In the case of a humanistic approach, Leaders and leading organisations have an obligation to look after the future of all people. People can decide for themselves how well organisations, governments, and leaders are currently fulfilling their obligations.

Unfortunately, business models do not focus on the future of humanity. In the case of seemingly innovative companies, responsibility ends if sales do not continue to increase, or profit suffers. Even where ecology and sustainability appear to be a priority, this is not always the case.

The internet is full of advertising and sales information, whereas contributions to human values and social concepts for the future are rarely mentioned.

In some communities, individuals do not even have a say in shaping their own future; somebody makes decisions for them. At best, these are people who have been voted by a majority and therefore have the power in their hands.

Young/old, women/men and other types of diversity

The world is full of diversity, this has come about without our help and will continue to exist. Our world would not exist without diversity / opposites and it would also not be so interesting.
However, opposites must be balanced or stabilised.

Discussing diversity is what distinguishes freedom and democracy. Yet in recent years, diversity have played an ever-increasing role. In discussions, stakeholders not only want to talk about related topics, but focus on asserting their positions. "Opposition for opposition's sake" is common and finding solutions often drags on unnecessarily long or is blocked.

The differences and the disputes to get better positions are not the main problem here, but rather the fact that the stabilising effect of similarities and existing dependencies are overlooked. We are initially all humans and only secondly different in one way or another.

Countries, nationalism, demarcations

Together, we humans have always congregated in communities. Long-term relationships, stakeholder groups, territorial groups and many more reflect our need for solidarity, as well as our desire for boundaries.

All these ways of coexistence have their own structures and rules. That is normal.

After all, a football team would not play according to volleyball rules and vice versa. If one team tries to impose its rules onto another, takes away its playing field or tries to gain advantages in other ways, this will almost certainly lead to conflicts.

This simple example makes it clear to everyone, how absurd it is to "enforce" their own rules onto others; however, this is exactly what happens between countries, religions, and ideologies, among others. This is not helpful and can even be dangerous.

If we humans understand and curb this absurdity, a great deal of energy would be freed up for constructive things.

Concentrations of power and monopolies

Diversity and competition are important for the development and resilience of societies. Concentrations of power and monopolies, however, lead to monoculture. Concentrations of power can be successful for a limited amount of time, but in the long-run they are inflexible and vulnerable.

Large companies can play an important unifying role, particularly where global understanding is concerned. However, their current focus is not on meeting social standards und global obligations, but predominantly on making a profit. But this could be changed – or not?

Even if many people call for strong leadership at times, concentrations of too much power should be avoided, in whichever form. History is full of examples, where concentrations of power have led to the oppression of communities or have even resulted in disaster.

If only one leader is in power, then problems arise as soon as this person is no longer in power. In many cases, no other person can become a suitable leader and a "leadership vacuum" occurs.

But many people need leadership. For this reason, the choice of leaders is of essential social interest.

Systematically relevant

Who or what is "systematically relevant"?

Up until the coronavirus pandemic, the term "systematically relevant" was strongly influenced by the financial crisis. In this way, stakeholder groups secured their social acceptance.

The pandemic has, however, shown what is really "systematically relevant" for us humans and hopefully this will result in in-depth discussions, analyses, and a shift in priorities.

This does, for example, concern the classification of groups of professions and their social acknowledgement. At first glance, there are contradictions between "systematically relevant", social recognition and current income.

A future concept should be designed to reduce or eliminate such contradictions.

Money, bitcoin, or the like

Money has a practical relevance; in that it facilitates the exchange of goods and services. Indirectly, money enables an estimation of the worth that goods and services have for society.

In the past decades, the system of "money" has been transformed into a financial economy. This created its own - no longer transparent - rules and encouraged the concentration of power. Financial products were created that do not generate any social value.

Money is not linked to one person or organisation; the possession of money does not change this. This freedom is both a blessing and a curse. Every attempt to get transparency of money flow and ownership is met with a workaround such as cryptocurrencies. Bitcoin etc. are, however, nothing more than new solutions for the old "money system". If aligning the finance system to people's needs again would succeed, then no new form of "money" would be necessary.

The technologies developed in connection with cryptocurrencies could possibly be used for the value/valuation system of »Humanity 10.0«.

The coronavirus pandemic

The outbreak of the corona (Covid-19) virus resulted in a world-wide pandemic. People died, supply chains were being disrupted, production came to a standstill and product shortages occurred. Travel and daily life are restricted.

The pandemic is a real "highlight", but is the term "highlight" inap-propriate? Are we not always on the lookout for "highlights" and do not appreciate the value of normalcy?
A minor virus has shown us our greatest weaknesses. Too often, we think that we have everything under control and that we are on top of things.

Under the pressure of the coronavirus pandemic, politicians were all suddenly united: "money should not be a problem". Whether or not the realisation that there are more important things than money was sincerely meant, will remain to be seen in future.
This focus on community and solidarity gives us reason to hope. We should build on that and follow up on all this food for thought. It depends on all of us if there are to be any lessons learned from the coronavirus crisis. We are well-advised to think carefully about sustainable long-term changes and the development of bold new concepts.

"Toilet paper egoism"?

People, communities, and organisations show their true colours in crises and when under pressure.

At the beginning of the coronavirus crisis, many people bought huge amounts of toilet paper. At first this seems to be irrational and pure egoism. You can neither eat toilet paper nor does your own consumption suddenly increase.

It is more difficult to keep a cool head and act rationally in situations where fear arises. There is a strong risk of being influenced by the actions of others.

Simultaneously, many people have suddenly and instinctively started thinking about what they might need in order to survive a crisis in future.

The lack of protective equipment, disinfectants, respirators, etc., have shown the importance of better planning by the whole of society, and more active preventive steps. We should join forces and support the decision-makers in such complex tasks in the best possible way and clearly convey what is important to us in the future.

Current trends

Trend: Extended lifespan

The desire to extend lifespan is presumably as old as humanity itself. There is nothing against the extension of worthwhile living time through, for instance, progress in preventive healthcare. To what extent immortality makes sense can be discussed at length. Behind the desire for immortality is perhaps the desire to increase one's own importance through an infinitely long life.

Looking around at people, it would already be an enormous step forward, if each one of us would give the limited life that we have a meaning. We should concentrate on that and invest less time in what are just dreams.
Immortality does not and will never exist.

Trend: Robots in all areas of life

Robots are finding their way into our lives in many ways and there is nothing to be said against the trend of making our life easier through machines. However, machines will not and should not be able to do everything for us. Sometimes it is wrong to rely on technological solutions.

The more robots or artificial intelligence play (AI) a role in our lives, the more closely crucial questions must be asked. In particular, what needs to be clarified is to what extent machines can make decisions about us humans.
This is already an intriguing question as far as medicine and autonomous driving are concerned. Regardless of what the future with robots and AI etc. brings, the focus of every machine should be to serve humans, all machines should be provided with a "code of conduct".

The term "digital twin" exists in the context of machines and robots; this refers to a digital copy of the respective machine or robot. With the help of this copy, processes, increased productivity, maintenance, and much more can be improved. In this way, even more can be gained from machines and robots.

Is not more and more data being gathered about us humans and "digital copies" being created?
Do we want to get even more out of every human being?

Trend: Warfare devoid of humans

Wars were and are absurd. Nevertheless, the story of humanity is a story of wars.
Currently there are still too many ongoing direct armed conflicts. More and more conflicts are also carried out on the internet. In almost all cases, it is not about defending human values, but rather about power and money.

If we fail to abolish wars, then we must address the issue of "killer robots". These emotionless automatic machines can potentially decide autonomously about human lives. However, automated attacks on vital infrastructures may even play a more important role in future. The fact that machines could make autonomous decisions about us humans makes no sense and poses a massive risk.

Investments in weapons only make sense, if they serve exclusively to protect people. However, this would require that the development, production and use of these weapons must be completely controlled by an organisation representing humanity.

The United Nations (UN) specifically founded, in order to control conflicts and weapons.
Unfortunately, we currently see the exact opposite of disarmament happening; an arms race in space is being considered – how absurd. We are already faced with the threat of the civil garbage resulting from space technology and we should be addressing this.

Trend: Artificial intelligence

Any intelligence, whether natural or artificial is helpful.
However, many questions still need to be dealt with in connection

with artificial intelligence.

Artificial intelligence, developed based on a variety of human experiences, will probably not pose a problem for humanity. "Superintelligence", however, which is artificial intelligence able to develop independently of the experiences of humans themselves, could well become a threat to us humans.

"Artificial intelligence" is an exciting trend, also because humans must determine in how far the logics should optimise our future processes. We must therefore take care that we do not become too dependent on parts of algorithms and ultimately lose our human identity.

Trend: Manipulation of genetic material

Human genes seem to have been decoded. Some of these findings are already being applied. Simple and natural "spare parts" will be available for people in a few years. This is good news.

In the context of this research, however, dangerous dreams of the creation of complete "humans" exist.

Humans have had to adopt to changing conditions throughout their existence and presumably their genes have changed as a result. Now we know what the actual state of our genes is, however, we do not know how and why our genes have changed over time. Another uncertain factor is our still-limited knowledge about the interactions and countless processes in our body and our dependence on environmental factors.

It is in fact, impossible for us humans to gain complete knowledge about ourselves. There will always be information missing, which is needed to understand us or to create fully "functioning" humans. Should we nevertheless want to produce human-like beings, many questions crop up, for example, what defines a human being? Do we know how we want to be – now and in the future?

Further issues

Trust

A new idea is hard to establish because there is no knowing whether it will be successful or not. On the other hand, new ideas have a kind of trust allowance.

Trust is of utmost importance to humans. It is so important that the actual issues to be trusted do not even play a role. We need trust because we need to feel secure or because we simply want to trust the status quo. Many people expect that everything will just go well. In most cases, the solution is not trust or hope, but rather courage and drive.

»Humanity 10.0« aims to establish trust and to stimulate action.

Respectable - starved

The combination of being "respectable" and "starving" should not really be an issue for us humans. Unfortunately, respectable people may sometimes even be at a disadvantage.

Most people know exactly what is meant by "good" and "bad" and "right" and "wrong", and what moral values represent. However, it is the communities/societies that determine which moral values prevail.

If you behave properly, you will not be punished. This is not always strictly correct but overall, common social practice. But is just "not being punished" enough to motivate?

No – there are many approaches to motivation, which use a system of rewards. Examples include collection systems, purchase bonuses, performance-based pay, promotion and many more. Looking at these motivation approaches, the appreciation of good overall social behaviour is scarce, even though we humans depend on the existence of "good", law and order, and moral values.

Why is there no "currency" for decency, morality, and promotion of the common welfare ...?

Digitalisation, Internet, and other tools

Digitalisation is currently being depicted as being the saviour of the 21st century – but what can it really do?

Digitalisation breaks down reality into small parts. This gridded reality including existing contexts can be processed more easily. New possibilities are evolving for influencing our real environment.

The image of a human being was first painted, then chemical substances were used for analogue photography. Many decades later, digital images of us were developed. In further decades or centuries, reality will be depicted differently, perhaps using quantum technology. Do we change by a changing image of ourselves?

The realisation that something must be done often culminates in the call for tools and other aids. These can be helpful, as well as being a good influence on developments.

Tools however, are, at the end of the day, only tools. The best tool is worthless, if you do not know what to do with it. Tools can be used for the benefit of us humans. At the same time, used wrongly, the same tools can cause a great deal of harm.

The internet offers many opportunities, for instance many people can be contacted quickly and simultaneously. But this does not directly change anything about reality or the fundamental behaviour of humans, which has been shaped over the centuries.

It is probably symptomatic of the Internet in 2020 that the first mail to the »Humanity 10.0« page was a spam mail with the goal of "hacking" or "making money".

Where do we go from here?

The examples selected in Part 1 offer a small taste of what is to come, i.e. what »Humanity 10.0« intends to focus on.

Based on the multitude of challenges and the complexity of the interrelationships, it becomes clear, which massive task a new concept for the future is faced with.

Each of us can probably find many more examples and potential for improvement within our own environment and can probably even come up with possible solutions.

At first glance, it seems almost impossible to find a suitable approach that can be implemented with all people.

In the next part, we will look at what is behind the approach of »Humanity 10.0«.

Part 2: »Humanity 10.0«

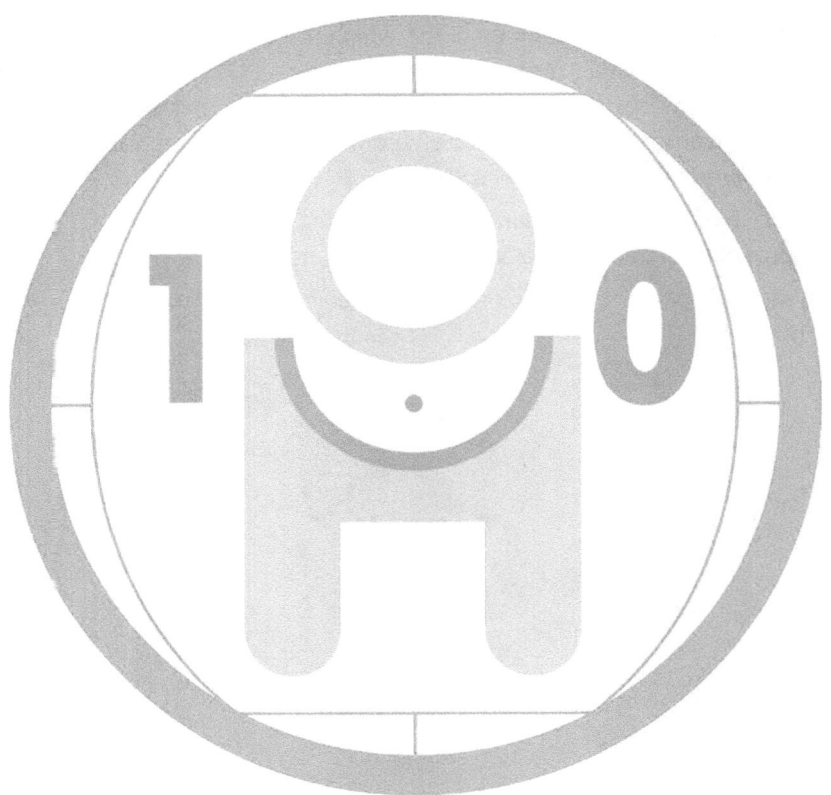

Visions

Visions give the future that extra something. They are the starting point for most discoveries and developments.

»Humanity 10.0« has the following visions:

- That People develop visions and goals together and define what is important for them;
- That governments implement people's wishes together with them;
- That changes are goal-oriented and coherent;
- That companies produce what is needed, sustainably;
- That dangers are recognised early on and undesirable developments are avoided;
- That provisions for crises are made in good time;
- That long-term satisfaction of all people is aimed for.

That we humans should be giving in-depth thought to our future is more of a necessity than a vision, but this sadly does not happen now.

Since all people live on the same earth, common goals and visions are necessary for survival. This does not mean that goals and visions must be the same all over the world.

Realising people's wishes by actively shaping the future is a clear vision. This should replace the trend of being "overrun by developments".

»Humanity 10.0« should enable a universal and sustainable approach, serving us humans. It should not be prone to attack due to its positive direction and make attacks on human values transparent, so that these can be easily overcome.

»Humanity 10.0« is very visionary because something seemingly impossible is being ventured.
However, »Humanity 10.0« could change many things for the better.

Goals

Visions cannot be realised without goals.
The more precise the goals, the easier it is to define the necessary steps to achieve them.

The **goals of** *»Humanity 10.0«* are to:

a) ***Ensure human survival***
   - Increase the bond between people.
   - Quickly find solutions to problems that threaten our existence.
   - Hold on to what is good and promote new things.

b) ***Develop society(ies)***
   - Strengthen moral values.
   - Ensure fair competition.
   - React intelligently to changes.

c) ***Increase people's satisfaction***
   - Introduce satisfaction as a separate criterion for all.
   - Set important and realistic goals for people.
   - Create freedom by ensuring clarity.

The individual goals culminate in the development of adaptable humanistic societies. These adaptable societies should evolve by using already- existing positive experiences, ideas, and solutions and by taking current shortcomings and mistakes into account objectively.

A new values and rating system, which is difficult to disapprove of, is to promote innovative strength by means of new incentives and to continuously improve what already exists.

Necessary changes will be addressed using open and dynamic rating criteria.

Principles

This chapter does not only deal with principles.

»Humanity 10.0« can be launched particularly well within certain framework conditions. In societies, these framework conditions are not always in place.

In order to establish convenient framework conditions, these must be well-known and coherent.

As mentioned at the beginning of the book, we assume that we operate independently in the reality which surrounds us, and that we can influence our lives within a certain framework. Even those who believe in external determination of people must accept the existence of reality. It is not important, whether thoughts occur freely or through "divine inspiration" by a higher power.

The thoughts are there and thus they represent reality.

In »Humanity 10.0«, the term "reality" amounts to "reflects reality". This is aligned with the general, as well as the scientific perception. Reality, not only encompasses scientific laws, but also what makes people tick.

Sometimes it is as though subjective and unrealistic interpretations of reality determine the way in which we do things. This is only possible if individuals or organisations have too much power. This allows them to further their own interests by manipulating people, by making false statements about reality, or even by using violence.

Subjective interpretations of reality do not have such serious consequences. If, for instance, a barrel is filled up to 50 % with water, there will be different opinions about the filling level. For some the barrel is "half full" and for others "half empty". Many evaluate the filling level as it is, at 50%.

All opinions represent reality and should be considered in the context of an overall concept. But who is right?

At the current moment in time, the filling level corresponds exactly to the measured 50%.

The interpretations "half full" and "half empty" can be ascribed to the person evaluating. Characteristics such as optimism and pessimism play a role, just as much as the emotional state of the person at the time.

The opinion "half full" could have been influenced by further information, such as the barrel could just be in the process of being filled. Thus, the interpretation could imply that the filling level could increase. The opinion "half empty", could arise, if the barrel has a large hole and there is no prospect of it filling up.

The following consequences can be drawn from this example for »Humanity 10.0«.

Reality not only consists of objective facts, but also the resulting different interpretations.

By forming an average opinion, subjective differences can be well compensated for.

Apparent interpretations, based on additional information are important for the future.

For »Humanity 10.0«, the objective reflection of reality and a systematic inclusion of trends are thus very important basic principles.

Working with current values, which are important for us humans, such as human rights, is a matter of course for »Humanity 10.0«. There is no doubt about this, despite keeping an open mind regarding all existing opinions. Considering diverse values does not alter the operation mode of »Humanity 10.0«.

The values themselves must be seen in a positive light by us humans only.

Discussions about values which are important for us humans have taken place in the past and are currently ongoing. Although, compared to their significance, we do not really concern ourselves with our values very much, or only selectively. And yet, it is important to find out the important values for every social development and to enforce them.

Future values should be specifically determined by the people themselves.

All values must be based on reality and must also be able to withstand the distant future.

The definition of values must neither follow subjective distortions of reality, nor should perceptions which are too pessimistic or idealistic dominate.

Values must be attainable, in order to develop a motivating force. Attacks on the values defined by people must be countered much more consistently than is currently the case.

The will to bring these issues more into the focus of public attention is an important general condition. Only then can »Humanity 10.0« help to protect and assert the values that serve people, to eliminate shortcomings and dissolve concentrations of power.

During the coronavirus crisis, it became very clear that the value of an issue can change according to circumstances. For a quick and optimal response to disasters, it would be helpful if there could be a social consensus about necessary measures. More attention should also be paid to the prevention, which is of great value. Therefore »Humanity 10.0« not only considers current trends and developments, but also extraordinary incidents.

There are innumerable observations to the questions surrounding our societies and important values by philosophers, politicians, and scientists from all disciplines, as well as other people from all walks of life.

The reflections of the modern philosopher, John Rawls are included in »Humanity 10.0« and adopted as a way forward. John Rawls' book "A Theory of Justice" includes interesting contexts and food for thought.

Just as they are for John Rawls, justice and equal opportunities are a central theme for »Humanity 10.0«.

The principle of "thinking in the original position" seems a good way forward for finding the "best social order".

Why the principle of "thinking in the original position" was chosen for the concept of »Humanity 10.0« and what its significance is, would take up many pages of this book, however, a short explanation is a must.

In the year 2020, we are certainly not in the "original position" of our human existence. However, if we look at the current situation of humanity, we will not find an established and convincing social construct for the coexistence of us humans, but a whole lot of different and partly contradictory models of society.
Individual societies exaggerate their advantages and significance for the world, mostly because they want to hold onto their status or get more power.

All previous approaches to social change have been unable to solve the many contradictions and challenges. Although scientific and technological developments are booming, the advancement of societies is not really progressing.
There are currently no relevant proposals for new societal models. Therefore, there is no reason why "thinking in the original position" should not be applied to further develop societies.

At this point, we want to look at which of John Rawls' thoughts may also be helpful and why.
The "veil of ignorance" is one such interesting approach. "Anything can happen to anyone" could be a suitable way of summarising this. The following example will illustrate the impact of the "veil of ignorance":

Three people must cross an unknown desert. They possess nothing but the clothes on their backs. After surviving the desert, they come into our normal current world and must, so to speak, "survive" all over again.
Six water cans at 10 litres and 6 gold bars at 20 kg are at the ready. Each person can take 2 two items with them.

The value of 40 kg of gold ensures a suitable fresh start and 40 kg are still manageable in terms of weight. However, since extremely dry and unknown terrain must be crossed and much water is provided, it must be assumed that a crossing of the desert without water is not possible.

Thus, hardly anyone will embark on a trip to the desert just with gold and without water, because the risk of dying of thirst is too high. The other extreme would be to take 2 cans of water. Both cans would initially be as heavy as the gold bars. After crossing the desert, nothing would be left.

Presumably and because of their "veil of ignorance", people will take 1 can of water and 1 gold bar with them. Thus, they instinctively follow the "Maximin-rule". This rule states that the compromise is the most likely optimal solution.

Until now, however, people had each decided for themselves. They could, however, cross the desert together, support each other and optimise what they take with them.

Should they, for example, take 5 cans of water and one gold bar with them, they almost maximise their chances of survival and simultaneously, they would have something with which to start a new life.

Perhaps 4 cans of water would also suffice, in which case, it would be possible to take 2 bars of gold.

When people get together to form a community, new opportunities and advantages arise. However, for this to happen, common decisions and rules are necessary.

This brings us to another important principle, that of "ethical preferences".

The community as the best provision can only function, if all its members have access to its advantages via common values and agreements.

Before the march through the desert, at least the use of the water and the division of the gold must be regulated and it must be clear that everyone feels bound by these rules.

Someone who completely ignores "thinking in the original position", because of his or her currently favourable life situation, could rapidly become very lonely in the "desert".

With the help of this example, it hopefully becomes clearer why
- the "veil of ignorance"
- the „Maximin-rule" and
- 'ethical preferences"
have been incorporated into the approach of »Humanity 10.0«.

Appropriate approaches play an important role for making the right decisions, when developing a concept for the future. Many decisions are made (too) spontaneously, emotionally with considerably simplified assumptions and according to instinct.

The Nobel prize winner, Daniel Kahneman investigated why people often do not think and act rationally. He discovered that there are two fundamentally different patterns of thinking. He published his findings in the book "Thinking Fast and Slow".

The first thinking pattern "fast thinking" is always active, it basically takes places automatically in the subconscious. This often must be simplified, because knowledge gaps cannot be filled at short notice. "Fast thinking" is important for everyone, when quick decisions must be made.

"Fast thinking" should be divided up again into intuitive and emotional thinking. While intuitive thinking is based on experiences and is relatively precise, emotional thinking is strongly dependent on the situation and mood and is therefore less suitable for making important decisions.

"Slow thinking", the second thinking pattern is seldom active. It must be consciously addressed.

The goal of "slow thinking" is to reflect reality as closely as possible. Uncertainties are usually eliminated using knowledge or algorithms. The logic used ensures traceability. The results can thus be used for later intuitive "fast thinking".

In many cases "Slow thinking" provides support for the "fast thinking" process. It is therefore contrary to what might be assumed, not always part of a planned process.

Due to the distinct system, "slow thinking" is often complicated and people are overwhelmed by it.

The advantage of "slow thinking" is the close consistency with reality.

Perhaps it is still not clear, why the use of correct thinking is so important. The following example serves to illustrate this.

Presumably all of us have, at some stage, seen a disaster movie. Let us reduce the plot to a group of people who find themselves in an exceptional situation (catastrophe). Existential decisions must be made.

Some of the people are completely overwhelmed. They are not capable of acting and hardly react at all, they cease to think.

A second group of people panics and makes emotional decisions. The people in this group often come to harm because of their partly irrational decisions. This corresponds to the emotional "fast thinking".

The group with experiences or the ability to draw unknown conclusions from what they have learned from known situations, will almost certainly make the correct decisions by means of intuitive "fast thinking".

And then there is the "hero". This person can activate the ability to "think slowly" in spontaneously occurring situations. He or she proceeds systematically, according to plan and the decisions made are usually the right ones. "Heroes" can switch to "slow thinking" quickly.

Thus, it would be obvious to favour "slow thinking" altogether. However, this is not that easy, because "fast thinking" is automated, partly in the subconscious, it cannot simply be turned off or exchanged for "slow thinking". Moreover, "fast thinking" is much more common than "slow thinking".

Where science is concerned, "slow thinking" is predominant. Since it is not readily available, it must be effectively planned and reinforced with intuitive components.

Particularly strategic decisions should reflect reality as far as possible. In this case there is no alternative to planned "slow thinking".

However, since "fast thinking" is more readily available, this should also be used where applicable.

This leads to a new principle for »Humanity 10.0«.
»Humanity 10.0« must consider both patterns of thought and apply them as effectively as possible.
Which way of thinking should be considered or used and when, is mentioned in the respective places in the book.

»Humanity 10.0« should provide impetus for many people from all walks of life. In addition, a basis for discussion will be proposed on how issues, as well as values can be rated and prioritised.

In the case of »Humanity 10.0«, much scientific input, as well as ideas for the many details will be necessary and implementation must be very well thought through.

Note:
Artificial intelligence will provide additional resources for "fast logical thinking" in the future. This is to the advantage of us humans if the logic used, reflects reality well.

Idea: Innovative values/rating system

In the previous chapters, we have looked at current challenges, identified the need for social change, as well as establishing appropriate visions and goals. Important principles and overall conditions for »Humanity 10.0« were compiled. Thus, we can now move to the idea for a new values/rating system.

The »Humanity 10.0« - values/rating system is designed to operate using a goal-oriented approach. Safeguarding and improving life for all people are the highest goals. Other goals and approaches described in the chapters "goals" and "principles" will constantly be strived for.

The values/rating system should be universally applicable to almost everything, to issues such as conditions, structures, situations, and trends, as well as persons, organisations, and relationships. The actual status of affairs, as well as foreseeable, possible developments are considered. Ideas for possible future changes are regarded as trends.

The values/rating system should incorporate as many framework conditions and contexts as possible, in order to clearly portray reality. Just this requirement could lead to a great deal of complexity.

The values/rating system should be future-proof, in other words, visionary, flexible and adaptable. This is the only way to ensure that it can be used over long periods of time.

The already-mentioned criteria can only be mastered if the process is understandable and acceptable for everyone.
The aim is for this to become the "smallest common denominator" with the greatest possible impact for us humans.

Obvious areas of focus

In order to keep things simple, it is necessary to focus on a few things only. These should be universally applicable and should help to serve the goals of »Humanity 10.0«.

What can the *obvious areas of focus* for a values/rating system like this be? The following approach is employed:

It is about the life of every single human being. Thus, it is clear, that we, as *human* beings are the decisive focus of the values/rating system.
We can somehow get by, but what is key in determining our quality of life are:

- Our close *surroundings*; and
- The *community* surrounding us.

Our future is only secured, if:

- Our entire *environment* is intact; and
- We act as one *humanity*.

The established areas of focus are illustrated in the following diagram.

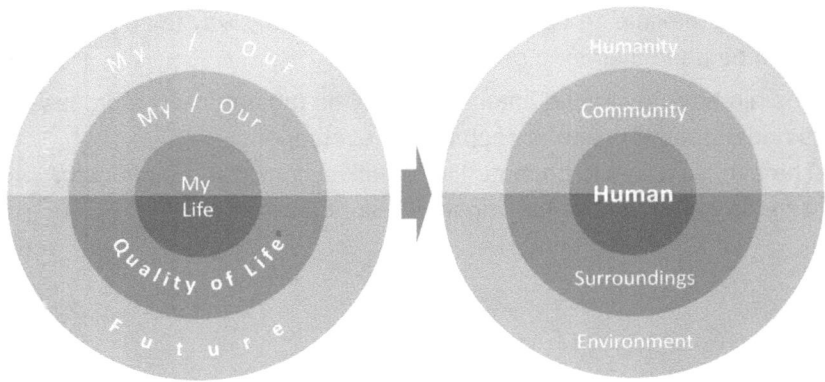

Figure 3: Establishment of the areas of focus

When the human takes centre stage, this could imply that »Humanity 10.0« has an egoistic approach. However, the other four areas of focus incorporate plants, animals, and natural resources etc. much more in the rating process than many other approaches.

As »Humanity 10.0« is supposed to be realistic, there is no way around looking at what it really is – somewhat egoistic.

These areas of focus consider both the ideational/social and the material/life-supporting needs.
They may seem to be somewhat abstract at first, not immediately tangible and consist of many different facets that may be interrelated. Therefore, further details on the areas of focus follow.

Human

There is no such thing as "the" human being.
We humans are very varied, have different characteristics and individual strengths and weaknesses. We are also very much influenced by our environment.
Despite these differences, we humans are predominantly similar.

Even if our chosen paths are different, we all want to live in dignity, be satisfied and we need a certain amount of security. In order to reach these goals, people allow themselves be motivated and are even prepared to change. Motivation is usually successful if it is beneficial. Thus, a further requirement arises: »Humanity 10.0« should offer each individual advantages.

Let us go back to the desert example from the chapter on principles and expand it to include the diversity of people.

One thousand people are to cross an unknown desert. They have nothing but the clothes on their backs. After crossing the desert, they return to today's normal world and must then - so to speak - "survive".
Two thousand cans of water containing 10 litres each and 2,000 gold bars weighing 20 kg each are at the ready. Again, each person may take 2 items with them.
What occurs as a result of the large number of people?

There are probably people who are more than willing to take a risk and dare to cross the desert with only 2 bars of gold. There will also be cautious people, whose highest priority in the desert is short-term survival; they take 2 cans of water with them.
The majority will probably go for the compromise and take 1 can of water and 1 gold bar, so that in total, the same number of water cans and gold bars will be taken.
Thus, although the individual approaches are different, again, the average remains the optimum.
So, when we talk about the priority "human being", the criteria which evolve for the "human" result from the averages of the characteristics of all people. Thus, we follow the "Maximin" rule, which represents the optimum.

The one thousand people could form a community for crossing the desert and benefit from the resulting advantages. The mutual decision, as well as the definition and enforcement of the rules becomes more time-consuming and difficult than in the case of the same scenario with 3 people, nevertheless, the advantages of the community are the same in both cases.

Since the events, issues etc. also follow the same principle of an average (normal) distribution, overall, there are no advantages for any extremes. In other words, those willing to take risks have no advantage over particularly cautious people and vice versa.
In the case of the priority "human", the average person will be considered for the purposes of the values/rating system of »Humanity 10.0«.

One thing should be noted.
Even if extremes have a certain appeal to us, we should stick to the average optimum. Most people cannot and should not follow extremes.
However, we can use extremes as an incentive to review our long-term average attitude and to correct it if necessary.

Community

Community did play a role in our example of people crossing the desert.

A community is primarily a group of people, such as a family, a club, or a religious community. Many groups are interest groups. Communities play a major role in life and have their own group dynamics.

A community in the sense of »Humanity 10.0« includes companies, authorities, political parties or even larger and global companies, the United Nations (UN) and the European Union (EU).

People are social beings and need communities.
However, communities are more diverse and complex than people. How can this area of focus still be used as a criterion?
Communities are like people because of their diverse interests and outlooks. An "average community" is based on the sum of all the different aspects of communities, in the same way as for people.

A healthy society finds its own balance. For example, left-wing and right-wing parties coexist. A government opinion usually goes alongside the opinion of the opposition. In physics, by the way, every force has a counterforce.
Even if a pendulum swings strongly in one direction, it is always corrected. Many years can go by between the swing in one extreme direction and the correction, in some cases in form of a catastrophe.

Communities and their rules are created by people and can there-fore be optimised by people.

Communities are not only a focus for »Humanity 10.0«, they are also subjected to rating by »Humanity 10.0«. In this way, individual communities can be prevented from adopting a dominant position in the values/rating system.

Humanity as a whole

The total number of all people from all communities constitutes the whole of humanity. During our daily life, we rarely think about humanity as a whole.

With this focus, necessary common visions, goals, and rules, which secure our survival as humans, should be considered. Humanity as a focus also serves the purpose of incorporating the things that people have in common so that the differences are not overrated.

»Humanity 10.0« can help to optimise the visions, goals, and rules, already determined for people.

Close surroundings

Even though globalisation has enabled goods from all over the word to play a major role in satisfying our material needs, our close surroundings still provide the basis for our lives.
Close surroundings include the natural resources that surround us, such as air, water, forests, animals, and man-made things, like cities, factories, and infrastructures. The natural resources of our close surroundings are, to a certain degree, directly related to the global environment.

Our close surroundings can be clearly perceived by each individual and we usually react directly to changes in our close surroundings, although not always proactively.

Parts of our close surroundings are significantly influenced by us humans. These parts are particularly interesting for rating by the »Humanity 10.0« - values/rating system. People can easily relate to the rating results and consequences.

The entire environment

We are directly dependent on natural resources, as well as functioning ecological systems. Unfortunately, we are not always aware of this. People are slowly, but not sufficiently, becoming aware of environmental protection. The reason for this is that negative impacts of "environmental sins" usually occur in the future.
As a result, the consequences for the entire environment, as well as close surroundings, must be directly included in the rating of issues, trends, and ideas.

Thus, the subject of environmental protection plays a role in the rating of each one of the areas being focussed on by »Humanity 10.0«. Time-consuming discussions about individual factors, such as pollutant limits, will not be dropped, but the pressure to comply with them will increase.

Relevance of the areas of focus

The areas of focus define our future priorities. They are the criteria on which the rating of issues and trends comes down to. As far as the importance of the areas of focus is concerned, the ideational/social focus, that is the community and humanity, seem to be less significant than the material /life-supporting focus via close surroundings and entire environment. However, that is a fallacy. If the commodities ensuring sustainment were distributed so unequally in the community that some people did not get their fair share, this has the same effect as if there were generally too few commodities available for that purpose.
In every war, people die because our similarities do not come across sufficiently. This is just as bad as people dying because of the destruction of our environment.
Is the choice of areas of focus of »Humanity 10.0« trivial – too unspectacular?

That would be a good sign because it means the areas of focus make sense and we would have achieved our goal of "simplicity".

Issues and trends

Issues can be for example:

- Manufactured products and services offered;
- Declarations of intent, statutes, programmes,
     such as party programmes;
- Relationships between people;
- Interdependencies between politics and economy;
- Relationships between states;
- People's actions, also everyday situations;
- Critical situations/states of affairs;
- Trends and developments, for example, global warming;
- ...

Which issues and trends should be rated?
Basically, everything can be rated.

Although, not all issues and trends are equally important. Not every area of focus has the same significance for every issue and trend. Therefore, a systematic approach and prioritisation is required for the rating of issues and trends.

In the first phase, many issues could be investigated, thought through and roughly rated, using the »Humanity 10.0« areas of focus. In this way, the issues and trends that are important will soon become apparent.
Particularly interesting are the trends and issues, which we, as humans, can influence/improve and where challenges are already apparent. A broad consensus would come about in these cases.

It may be that currently no consensus on objective criteria and ratings is possible because, for instance, extreme ideologies may deny change. In these cases, a quantitative approach does not make sense. However, who is hindering, how and why should be transparent.

It is also an asset to define exemplary issues early on, which will then be subjected to further quantitative rating, during the first phase. Details on the procedure for introducing »Humanity 10.0« will be provided in the following chapters.

How can we choose the right issues and trends from the vast number though? Firstly, we look at the question: "Which trends and issues do people find interesting?"

We are usually interested in things that contribute to satisfying our needs. If we want to involve all people, then we must proceed by meeting their needs.

"Maslow's hierarchy of needs" illustrates the correlations between people's needs and their personal development in a simplified form, see the following figure (Source: *https://en.wikipepia.org/wiki/Maslow%27s_hierarchy_of_needs*).

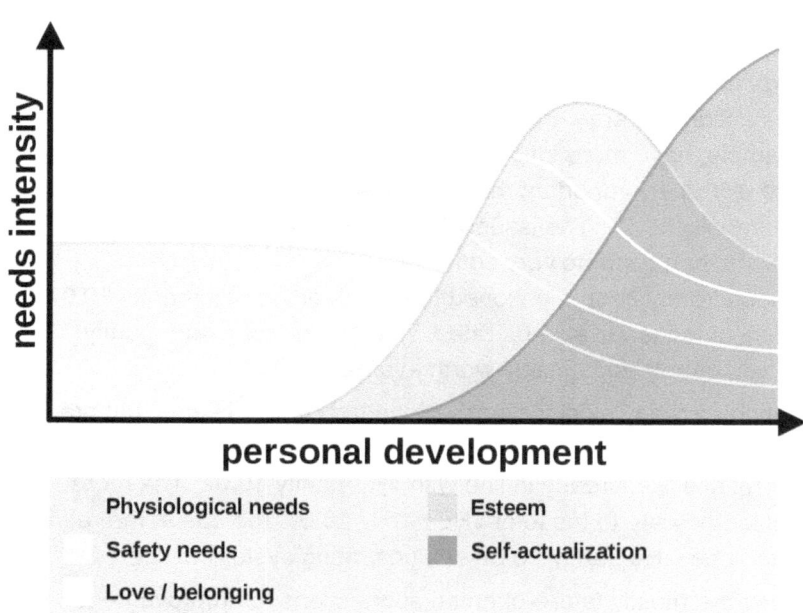

Figure 4: Dynamic illustration of the hierarchy of needs

The fundamental idea is that first the basic needs, i.e. physiological, safety and social needs are (must be) satisfied, before a person addresses (can address) self-actualisation needs. Although this model seems to be relatively simple, it should be applicable for the 'average person" and thus sufficient for our purposes.

As can be seen in the image, the basic needs play a role in each of the personal development steps. This means that regardless how differently people and societies develop, securing the basic needs is essential. Hence, the trends and issues that secure basic needs have the highest priority.

Since the basic needs of many key players and decision-makers are satisfied, their needs are rather of the individual, self-fulfilment kind. Thus, trends and issues that enable these needs to be satisfied must also be considered. Ideally, the selection of trends and issues will motivate key players and decision-makers to satisfy the basic needs in their societies.

Organisations play a special role.
The actions of large organisations, especially political parties, for example, have more influence than those of individuals. It is therefore extremely important that organisations are rated according to »Humanity 10.0«. The issues, trends and ratings affecting organisations, can become very complex.
It has already been mentioned that parts of the »Humanity 10.0« - areas of focus will also be rated. Whether or not a community serves people is definitely worth evaluating.

Ratings already exist for many of the trends and issues that are dependent on the chosen areas of focus/criteria. In many cases, the ratings are already in line with »Humanity 10.0«. The more similar they are to those of »Humanity 10.0«, the easier the rating in the new »Humanity 10.0« - values/rating system will be.

Ideas are mostly future-oriented suggestions for improvement. It is worthwhile to include them early on as possible trends in the rating. The potential ideas should be evaluated, particularly when there are no foreseeable trends for a particular issue or the foreseeable development is not satisfactory.

The presentation and rating of issues, trends and ideas must be objective and fact-based.
Reality should be portrayed in the best possible way.
In this phase, links to a particular person or organisation are deliberately (still) not an issue, because respective sensitivities can hinder ideas and objective solution-finding.

The general procedure per issue will be described in more detail in the next chapter.

Procedure per issue/trend

The main idea behind »Humanity 10.0« is to achieve improvements in as many issues and trends as possible.

Since the focus is on medium- and long-term improvements, dealing with history is not a priority. Past experiences are, of course, considered in the rating.

Attribution of blame for shortcomings or the like to people or organisations is not considered while looking at issues/trends.

Essential steps while considering issues and trends are:

1. Stimulating reflection, initial assessments.
2. Collecting ideas for improvements.
3. Considering contexts.
4. ***Using »Humanity 10.0«- areas of focus as rating criteria for the current status.***
5. ***Using the rating criteria to assess the impact of known developments and ideas.***
6. Defining common goals and finding solutions.
7. Implementing idea(s) and monitoring progress.

In addition to the usual reflection on issues important for the future, the »Humanity 10.0« - values/rating system is applied no later than during steps 4. and 5.

Following are some remarks on the steps.

Re. 1. Stimulating reflection, initial assessments

Everybody should think before expressing opinions or acting. Since this is not always the case, it is generally a good idea to stimulate reflection.

It is by no means easy to incorporate objective rating and contexts into this process. This is, however, essential in order to be able to make a realistic decision.

What really helps are structured initial ratings. Individual aspects are thus not only thought through, but a rough rating is made as to whether they are positive or negative or whether such impacts can be expected.

Systematic "slow thinking" would be a good choice while reflecting. But, when thinking about issues for the first time, "fast thinking" is very common and can also be very useful.

Re. 2. Collect ideas for improvement

It is always best to collect ideas early on and not to rate them immediately one by one. In this way, trends and suggestions for improvement can already be identified.

Thus "fast thinking" would almost be preferable for the collection of ideas. We are all familiar with this in the context of brainstorming. When sufficient ideas can be rated, it is easier to highlight the most productive amongst them.

Nowadays, many ideas have a commercial character.
»Humanity 10.0« aims to increasingly incorporate non-commercial ideas. These are possibly of much greater social benefit. In addition, the visibility of community engagement can be increased.

Short-term ideas solve current challenges. Mid- and long-term ideas should not be underestimated; they can often be much more sustainable and more efficient.

For the development of the values /rating system itself, long-term and sustainable ideas, as well as systematic "slow thinking" are needed.

Re. 3. Consider contexts

Ideas and concepts are often fixated on a certain area. Contexts are either not sufficiently considered or deliberately ignored. Many ideas and concepts still manage to gain acceptance through efficient marketing. Many calculations to estimate the benefits are solely business-based and not economy-based and certainly not for the purpose of all people on earth. Profits are gladly taken and the general public is then expected to pick up the costs for damage to the environment or health.

A fundamental rethink is the only way to change this situation. This rethink is partly already happening and sustainability is playing an increasingly prominent role. There is, however, a great deal of potential for improvement.

Considering as many contexts as possible is tedious and time-consuming, which is why »Humanity 10.0« wants to initiate reflection at an early stage and not when problems are already acute. If we concentrate on the important things, we have more time to consider contexts and optimise solutions.

The current outlook on constant quantitative growth is no longer tenable. An improvement in quality is necessary and sensible in many areas. Good quality is satisfying, it protects the environment and secures our existence.
High quality standards are also needed for considering contexts and with »Humanity 10.0« generally.

Re. 4. Assessing the current status

Objectively correct and transparent assessments, are not always easy to achieve. On the one hand, necessary information is often initially missing, on the other hand, reality is often distorted.
To obtain as much correct information as possible, is one of the exercises of the third step, where as many contexts as possible should be considered. Time and resources are limited, however, there are various ways of achieving proper assessments.

Quick assessments can be statistically evaluated and the results used. Or, alternatively, a lot of information can be collected, allowing few information gaps and sufficient time for intensive thought. We certainly use both.

This is where a principle of »Humanity 10.0« comes into play. The decision criteria have been kept simple with the 5 defined areas of focus. In this way "fast thinking", as well as "slow thinking" can be included in the assessment of the selected issue/trend. This allows many more perspectives to come to light and corresponds to our normal way of thinking.

A note on the procedure:
At first questions are asked about how the chosen issue affects the 5 areas of focus.
The situation, status, activity... positively or negatively affect:

- Humanity as a whole;
- Community;
- Humans;
- Close surroundings; and
- The entire environment.

The answers are collected. In order to be able to make precise assessments, a quantification is necessary.
This results in a further intermediate step; suitable gradations must be chosen for the quantification.
For example, as shown in the figure: "Assessment of the current situation", 3 negative and 3 positive gradations can be chosen.
This has the advantage that a neutral level exists at the same time. If an area of focus has no significance, it can thus be assessed as not relevant (neutral).

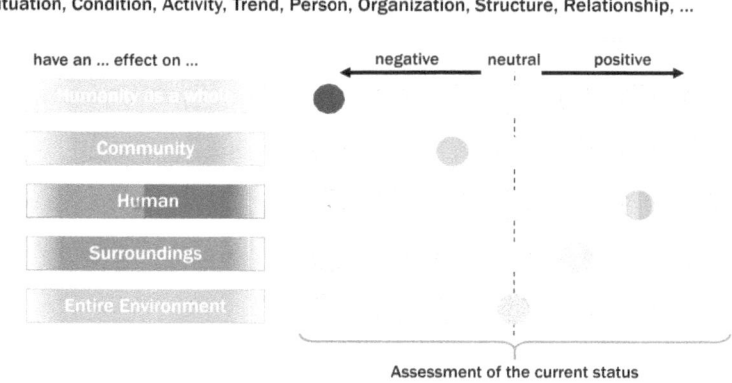

Figure 5: Assessment of the current status

It may be possible that the chosen assessment gradations do not fit the actual issue. The gradations must then be adjusted again.

Ultimately, the goal is to obtain the best possible assessment for the respective issue.

Re. 5. Assessing developments and ideas

The actual status of an issue is not always decisive but the future changes in the issue can be more important. This is also considered accordingly in the »Humanity 10.0« - values/rating system.

The procedure is like that of the current rating of an issue, the only difference being that further ratings are made of the possible future status. For this purpose, a timescale of xx-years in the future should be chosen.

In contrast to the assessment of the current status, the assessment of future developments cannot be based on existing data. It could happen, that reflection on future developments first must be initiated. Whether well-informed statements can ultimately be made, depends on the issue itself. Despite all the difficulties, however, predictions can be extremely valuable, especially in influencing trends at an early stage.

As can be seen in the following figure: "Assessing developments", the trend per area of focus is of interest.

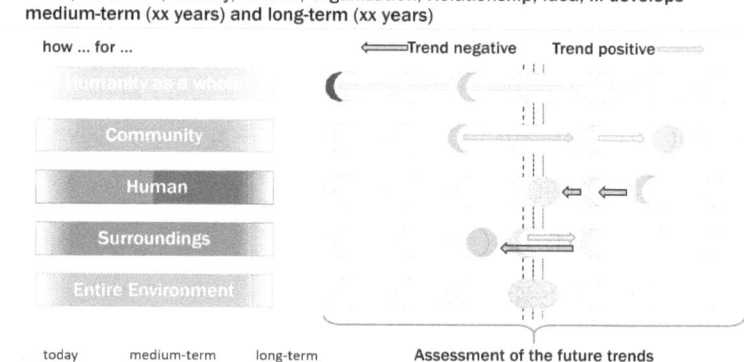

Situation, Condition, Activity, Person, Organization, Relationship, Idea, ... develops
medium-term (xx years) and long-term (xx years)

how ... for ...   ⟸Trend negative   Trend positive⟹

Humanity as a whole

Community

Human

Surroundings

Entire Environment

today   medium-term   long-term   Assessment of the future trends

Figure 6: Assessing developments

An issue may be rated as being positive, however, it is developing negatively. This information is important to be able to take justified preventive measures.

Ratings of the current status are already helpful. But, for a future concept, such as »Humanity 10.0«, trends are probably even more important.

Only scientifically-based work ("slow thinking"), combined with a lot of computing power and with the inclusion of "artificial intelligence" will lead to optimal results in the assessment of trends.

Re. 6. Defining common goals and finding solutions

When the actual status of an issue is clear and how it is likely to develop, concrete solutions for improvements can be considered.

Solutions can arise spontaneously via "fast thinking", as well as via systematic "slow thinking". Which solution is ultimately chosen is an important decision-making process. This must be well-founded and the solutions must be logical and sustainable. Quick-fix solutions would not be suitable, "slow thinking" is necessary.

The interests of individuals and organisations play a role at the latest by the time the final choice of solutions is made. This can lead to delays and jeopardize an impartial rating. If a solution is found to be objectively correct, however, no person or organisation will permanently oppose it. If extreme obstructions or excessive delays occur, alternative solutions should be considered.

Re. 7. Implementing idea(s) and monitoring progress

The ideas, or rather potential solutions must be implemented. Monitoring progress is also vital.

This is no different for »Humanity 10.0«-rated solutions than for any other form of implementation. There are sufficient experience and numerous tools available.
During this phase, creativity and ideas concerning high efficiency are always welcome.

The values/rating system

The values/rating system, was already mentioned in the previous chapter "Procedure per issue/trend" in the sections "Re. 4. Assessing the current status" and "Re. 5. Assessing developments and ideas".

Since the exact details of how the »Humanity 10.0« - values/rating system could be structured are not crucial for the overall under-standing, this part has been added as Appendix 1. "Details on the values/rating system".
Some aspects of the values/rating system are described here to help understand what is behind it.

The values/rating system of »Humanity 10.0« consists of two parts.

The first part comprises the qualitative rating of issues, trends and ideas using the »Humanity 10.0« areas of focus as rating criteria. This was already described in the previous chapter. The qualitative rating provides a good overview and helps to ascertain the important issues, trends, and ideas.

As well as being practised, the values/rating system should, however fulfil still further functions. This is possible if the rating of issues, trends and ideas leads to a quantification. Precisely this quantifica-tion is described in Appendix 1. "Details on the values/rating system". At this stage, some key elements are mentioned.

There are five issues/trends per area of focus:

- Humanity as a whole;
- Community;
- Humans;
- Close surroundings;
- The entire environment.

The significance of the areas of focus for the respective issue/trend is brought into a suitable perspective by means of factors.

A rating is carried out for each of the five areas of focus for the:

- Current situation;
- Mid-term development; and
- Long-term development.

Factors are also foreseen for the rating dates, in order to be able to vary their significance.

Since the importance of the issues/trends for societies varies, they must be coordinated with one another; there are further factors for this purpose.

Priorities change as a result of exceptional situations, such as the coronavirus pandemic. This affects both the areas of focus for rating, as well as the rating dates. These changes are also adjusted via factors.

This short description already indicates that it is not easy to achieve genuine quantified and usable ratings. The development of the final rating mechanism is something that will occupy many experts. We can, however, assume that this is not an insurmountable task. There will be a values/rating system, that will provide quantified assessments of which facts/trends are important to us.

Generally valid value units arise, since the specific values of the areas of focus/trends are arranged in relation to each other. These will be called »Humanity Points«.

The possible results of the ratings are clarified again in the following examples.

Very important and positively-rated areas of focus/trends are awarded a lot of »Humanity Points«.

As already described in the previous chapter, neutral ratings are possible. There are no points for ratings which show a lack of importance.

Consequently, negative »Humanity Points« are also possible in the suggested values/rating system. As a result, very important and negatively-assessed areas of focus/trends are awarded many negative »Humanity Points«.

All other ratings lie somewhere between these two positive and negative extremes. Areas of focus can, therefore, be awarded positive or negative »Humanity Points«.

By the time the quantified rating is clear, it is obvious, which areas of focus/trends are decisive for us, as humans, and therefore must have priority.

If areas of focus/trends have a certain value in the form of »Humanity Points«, further applications arise. The most important application is to link the areas of focus/trends to persons and organisations.

One example should clarify the above.

A company meets an environmental threshold. This environmental threshold is the area of focus. The rating of the current status only reveals the fulfilment of the specifications, thus neither a positive, nor a negative rating; no »Humanity Points« are awarded in this case.

The company invests, in order to reduce pollutants. Within the mid-term rating period, the pollutants are reduced by 30% and in the long-term by 50%. The company is thus rewarded »Humanity Points« for the mid-term and long-term improvements.

Several positive effects ensue.

The main effect is the reduction of pollutants. Since it is clear that »Humanity Points« are only awarded for positive achievements, the public reputation of the company is improved.

»Humanity Points« also represent a value. It makes sense to recognise this socially, for example by facilitating investment.

The promise to keep to the mid- and long-term goals is monitored.

Let us consider this case in our current environment. From a business point of view, it makes no sense to invest. The threshold is already being fulfilled. If there are no changes in thresholds, which result in penalties, the companies do not invest. Investments would "not pay off".

Linking »Humanity Points« with persons and organisations has definite advantages.

Persons and organisations can be compared more objectively and competition is well known for stimulating business and promoting developments.

If th s competition is backed by a well thought-through and transparent values/rating system then people's trust will also increase.

»Humanity Points« are new, so further interesting aspects arise as a result.

»Humanity Points« can be put into use immediately for newly defined or prioritised social goals.

»Humanity Points« are only accrued in the case of positive effects for people. Each »Humanity Point« also has a direct, corresponding social equivalent. Therefore »Humanity Points« cou d be used as a kind of future "added-value currency".

The persons/organisations that have acquired »Humanity Points« can "exchange" these. People could, for example, redeem »Humanity Points« for important positions or exclusive social benefits. The possible advantages for organisations are very dependent on the kind of organisation.

Let us look at a further advantage of »Humanity 10.0« based on the following example.

According to calculations so far, the required CO_2 reduction targets will probably not be reached. In order to be able to achieve the targets, the industrialized countries would have to cooperate, without exception, to reduce their energy consumption by more than 50%. A specially tailored incentive system is beneficial.

So far, however, trade with "air pollution certificates" has not had the desired effect. There is a lack of will to put an appropriate price on air pollution, as well as the immediate involvement of all those concerned.

Air pollution is not our only problem; the oceans are full of plastic waste; soil is contaminated and much more.

Do we really want to provide a separate solution mechanism for each human problem? Can we expect people to constantly have to deal with new problems and with various methods of dealing with them? Or would not a holistic approach, such as the »Humanity 10.0« - values/rating system, be the better alternative?

The opportunities and advantages of »Humanity 10.0« and the values/rating system will be investigated in more detail during the book.

Despite the euphoria and optimism surrounding potential solutions, we should not lose sight of possible abuse; this will always exist. We do, however, have sufficient experience with other systems, to be able to take precautions, and if necessary, to apply effective sanctions.

»Humanity Points« and other values

The quantitative rating of an issue depicts the significance of that issue for us. If that significance is major, it results in many »Humanity Points«. A system of scaling is used, in order to be able to compare different issues with each other. The values/rating system will be set up in parallel to everything that already exists. It can be developed in a consistent manner and will function. However, the »Humanity 10.0« - values/rating system would then be one of many values/rating systems.

Most values/rating systems are created for selected purposes with specific rating criteria, for example for evaluating products or services and "like-buttons", as used in social media.
What is rated here, are issues, in the sense of »Humanity 10.0«. However, the current ratings do not always follow clear and objective criteria.
For example, "likes" are sometimes very subjective assessments. The relevance of a single "like" has become insignificant; only a mass of likes really makes an impact.
Other negative spin-offs of existing "values/rating systems" are slander and "shitstorms" or massive amounts of "dislikes".
These often lead to distress and psychological problems for those concerned.

How refreshing a values/rating system would be, with clearly defined criteria!

Some of the existing values/rating systems can sometimes be used for »Humanity 10.0«. The benefit of others, or to what extent they can be adapted, must be considered. It is particularly important to pay attention to goal-oriented and transparent criteria.

There are several comprehensive social values/rating systems, for example, political and economic systems, religious groups, and ideological trends. In the same way as »Humanity 10.0«, these are focussed on a multitude of topics. Unfortunately, these systems and partly their values and criteria are not compatible with each other.

The competition for people resulting from these social systems causes conflicts. Competition itself is not a bad thing.
However, in the process, too many values and rules which serve people, are not considered.

The question arises as to the relationship between the »Humanity 10.0« - values/rating system and the other values/rating systems.

The values/rating system of »Humanity 10.0« is a new and open system. This means that there are (still) no irrevocable values and rules. This creates the possibility to develop a fact-based tolerance. It is not "about the principle" but about solutions for people.
The »Humanity 10.0« - values/rating system enables us to generate a truly new view of the world.
»Humanity 10.0« focusses on the issues and the future. Historical events and ideologies etc. play a secondary role.
The »Humanity 10.0« - values/rating system is open to other values and rating systems; for example, belief "in a higher power" is not a criterion, but it also cannot be ruled out that belief and religious rules can be helpful.

Although the »Humanity 10.0« - values/rating system is open and flexible, it is clear, which values are important. The values must serve people's needs.
The alignment of the values is determined by the 5 areas of focus and implemented by open questions.

Is the situation, the status, the activity, the idea ...
positive or negative for
- Humanity as a whole,
- Community,
- Humans,
- Close surroundings, or
- The entire environment?

Basically, »Humanity 10.0« does not invent any new values;
the question if existing values have a positive or negative effect is analysed and rated. Existing values and rating systems are therefore directly or indirectly influenced.

In the sense of »Humanity 10.0«, existing values/rating systems, as well as »Humanity 10.0« will help to stimulate competition so that existing systems develop further. While non-sustainable values become less significant, positive values are strengthened.

»Humanity 10.0« has the potential to strengthen connections between people and to specifically promote positive develop-ments with its values/rating system.
It is suitable to serve as a unifying, lowest common denominator and connecting factor for the many different social systems and communities.

In case anyone should miss money as a value, perhaps this thought can help: Money itself has no objective value. Money serves as a tool to enable the exchange of goods, services, and actual values. Money even allows genuine human values (such as morals) to be bought and sold. Everyone knows how money is often linked to murder, bribery, oppression and much more. This is possible because money has no moral obligations.

Not everyone will immediately agree with the message that money has no value. But let us go back to the "desert example" in the chapter, "Principles"; a sack full of money would not be able to quench thirst in the desert.

The coronavirus crisis is also a good example of how money only, at best, has a relative value.
Billions of euros and dollars were "pumped into the market" every month. Individuals and organisations determined and continue to determine the distribution of money, at their own discretion.
This is not the only way in which money is relativised even on the highest level. Apart from that, the "fresh money" is mostly immedi-ately used for speculation purposes on the capital market.
Humanity experienced an absolute low and the stock exchanges hit new highs – how perverse!

»Humanity Points« can be used as a kind of benefit-oriented alter-native currency. They can only be accrued, if issues are clearly positive for humans and the environment. There is a genuine countervalue for each »Humanity Point« accrued.

Nowadays, if the money-printing machines are quickly started up, instead of a countervalue, the money already in circulation is devaluated. This is particularly problematic because people who like to save and go easy on resources are "punished".

»Humanity Points« can be linked to moral values via the selected criteria.

This should not only be of interest for us humans, but also for many organisations.

Different aspects of »Humanity Points«

Before »Humanity Points« can be linked to persons and organisations, some aspects need to be clarified.

A values/rating system, based on "handshake recognition" can only function well under certain circumstances. In the long run, few people will want to make sacrifices, without, at least, the prospect of recognition.
If strong motivation is a prerequisite for all groups of people and effects are also expected to be achieved quickly, solutions are required, which offer a countervalue, or rather a kind of award.
During the last decades, we have focussed very much on countervalue-systems.
One can argue whether this was (is) a good development, but there is no getting around the current expectations of a broad mass of people. If we look around in our life a bit, there are many, partly hidden, already existing reward and countervalue mechanisms.

The »Humanity 10.0« - values/rating system does not appear to be a countervalue-system at first glance. It will show what is positive and what is negative for us humans. The results of these ratings can themselves lead to insights and trigger reactions. »Humanity 10.0« promotes transparency and goal orientation. These effects already represent values for societies.

Implementing the consequences gained from the »Humanity 10.0« qualitative insights, remains the task of the existing values/rating systems.
However, as soon as quantitative ratings of the »Humanity 10.0« - values/rating system are available, many different possibilities arise.

Since »Humanity 10.0« is a future concept for all people, all the different and, in some cases, contradictory (positive and negative) characteristics of us humans must be considered.
In order to involve as many people as possible, the »Humanity 10.0« - values/rating system will have a reward and countervalue element. Whoever actively contributes to the creation of value for us humans,

should (be able to) receive an equivalent in the form of »Humanity Points«. Why be able to receive?

Those who want to contribute to society solely for moral or personal reasons are, of course, welcome to do so. The receipt of »Humanity Points« can be refused. But maybe it would be even better, to give acquired points to other charitable organisations.

The last point already brings us to the midst of the considerations on how »Humanity Points« can make a difference, and how and under which circumstances they are linked with other values. Promoting transparency and lessons learned, is already an interaction. Furthermore, in the case of »Humanity 10.0«, values from other systems are also judged according to whether they have positive or negative effects for us humans.

However, what is the quantifiable relation between »Humanity Points« and other values?

How are the »Humanity Points« linked to the stakeholders, individuals, and organisations?

»Humanity Points« for persons / organisations

Considering the following, we assume that the »Humanity 10.0« - values/rating system provides meaningful and objectively correct ratings and that the »Humanity Points« have an appropriate social countervalue.

»Humanity Points« can be linked with persons and organisations, when it is clear, how many can be awarded for which output. Individuals or organisations can be awarded »Humanity Points« by providing necessary services or fulfilling certain criteria.

A voluntary-based system would be particularly welcome in the introductory phase.

Persons and organisations could, for example, collect »Humanity Points«, in order to:

- Work specifically for the benefit of people;
- Present the services they have rendered to society; or
- Improve a negative image.

And in case countervalues are already defined:

- To receive services from society; or
- To be able to perform a high rank in society.

The success of voluntary-based systems is, for the large part, dependent on the extent to which motivation is convincing. Thus, attractive rewards are a must when things are done on a voluntary basis.

Unfortunately, the voluntary approach does not always go down wel, thus a further scenario plays a role, which functions based on concrete specifications.

It could be conceivable that an organisation must achieve a minimum amount of »Humanity Points«. This could be confirmed by a form of certification. Organisations are familiar with such systems. For example, ISO standards define the procedure and the rating criteria for management systems and environmental certification. If such a way forward is chosen for »Humanity Points«,

organisations should be able to handle it. However, the prerequisite is that implementable rating criteria are in place.
Mandatory systems can enable a higher level of pressure to be able to achieve certain goals faster.

A mandatory certified system is certainly not suitable for individuals and would not be in line with the principles of »Humanity 10.0«. Nevertheless, it is conceivable that a minimum of »Humanity Points« must be achieved in order to be able to carry out important social functions in important organisations. Since achievements must be genuine, the respective function would even be up-graded.
Another general statement about the rating of persons: The »Humanity 10.0« - values/rating system, mainly evaluates the issues, trends, and ideas, important for us humans. Even though the issues and trends, which are decisive for societies, are very much influenced by organisations, the allocation of »Humanity Points« to people is important. The more people and organisations participate in »Humanity 10.0«, the greater the positive effects.

Many people are daunted, when it comes to ratings, although they are happening continually. People participate in organised competitions, which are based on ratings. "Likes" on the internet and the rating of professional achievement are taken for granted. Even comparisons in the private sphere are continually being made.
In any case, well-founded and regulated ratings are definitely a better solution than anonymous estimates, shitstorms, and mobbing.

If establishing the »Humanity 10.0« - values/rating system as a trustworthy system based on facts is successful, further positive effects could follow.

In Part 3. of this book, the modus operandi, and mechanisms of »Humanity 10.0« are explained in more detail, using examples. The next chapter looks at the way that the framework conditions for »Humanity Points« can be shaped.

Organising »Humanity Points«

Even if it is not easy, we can almost certainly agree on the issues important to us and quantify these according to their significance. We have sufficient experience in handling ratings and point systems to enable a functioning mechanism for the accrual of »Humanity Points«. An isolated application, however, is neither realistic, nor does it make sense. Additional thought will be necessary for the »Humanity 10.0« - values/rating system, with respect to further contexts.

Since money plays a role in many points systems, the question automatically arises as to how »Humanity Points« and money relate to each other?
The answer is not that straightforward and dependent on how boldly we want to introduce »Humanity Points«. One thing is clear - »Humanity Points« will neither be able to, nor do they want to, replace money. In any case, money itself is not the problem, but the unequal distribution of money and property.

Firstly, let us consider who the accrued »Humanity Points« belong to. Every person or organisation, awarded »Humanity Points« for achievement owns these points. That is straightforward and to be expected. However, there are innumerable further interrelations, which must still be clarified. Some of these are subsequently looked at more closely.

»Humanity Points« are accrued based on the rating of issues, trends, and ideas. The value of a »Humanity Point« is the same for all persons or organisations.
Thus, not only an exchange of »Humanity Points« between persons or organisations would be easy to imagine, but »Humanity Points« could also be transferred from persons to organisations or vice versa.
Only – do we want that?

It would be conceivable that two types of »Humanity Points« exist; one type for persons and another for organisations.

Both types cannot be exchanged or transferred between the groups. This makes ratings easier; there is no need to compare the performance of individuals and organisations with one another.

If »Humanity Points« were to be linked exclusively to a person or organisation, having delivered the required achievement, a very secure values/rating system would result. It would not be possible for persons and organisations to take away »Humanity Points« from others. The experience and the necessary technologies for such a system already exist.
In the case of an exclusive link of »Humanity Points« with persons or organisations, further, interesting aspects arise. For example, »Humanity Points« could be cancelled in the case of a person's death or the disappearance of an organisation. In this way, there would be no inflationary effects of »Humanity Points«.
In addition, each person or organisation would have to take the trouble to acquire their own »Humanity Points« and could not " inherit" these without achievements of their own. The above-mentioned points would lead to a very fair solution. Those who achieve, profit from the system – if they "exist". There would be a distinct and positive difference to money. There seems to be no decisive factor for a solution of this kind.
The described solution is a new and relatively standalone way of dealing with »Humanity Points«.

Let us bring money back into the picture.
Many people will want to hold on to historical "achievements". Despite the fact, that the ongoing existence of money and previous possession of it is not being questioned, lots of people will initially reject the introduction of »Humanity Points« for fear or of the above or convenience. There are not many valid arguments for rejection, but we must deal with this possibility. Let us take a closer look at these challenges.

A major difficulty arises from the fact that many of those who possess power and property do not want to part with them. Although, this statement is only partially true. If we remember the aspects of personal development in the chapter "Issues and trends", perhaps the only thing missing is an opportunity or motivation for personal development.

There are many examples, of rich and powerful people remembering that they are part of a large community, which they must also contribute to. Accruing »Humanity Points« and thus demonstrably doing something for society, is perhaps worthwhile after all and definitely a way of further developing personality.

Of even more interest than those people who are rich and powerful is, however, the group of people who have received a small slice of the pie and see themselves as being "rich" because they can afford something now and again. However, when they consider their real power, this is quickly put into perspective again. This large group comprises many millions of people. They have mainly worked for their property. This group creates a great deal of value for societies and would presumably be the most beneficial for »Humanity 10.0«.

For most people who possess (too) little, »Humanity 10.0« provides significant benefits. Within the new values/rating system, they would suddenly have a truly equal position. Nobody would have »Humanity Points« to begin with and the same criteria for their acquisition would apply for all.

An equivalent value of society for a certain amount of »Humanity Points« could be a kind of "basic security". That could be a way of motivating the large group of people who have (too) little to become more involved in society.

They could find a sense of purpose and even start anew.

In turn, society would have the advantage of being able to "reach out" to this group again.

But back to the present and to the "power" of money. Regardless of whether there is agreement on this point, the gap between rich and poor must decrease again, to eliminate social tensions.

Talking of the money system, this would have to be transferred from rich to poor. Is this a realistic scenario? What would the rich gain in giving their money to the poor on a large scale?

»Humanity 10.0« could provide the required motivation for that to happen. When rich people give their money to the poor, they acquire »Humanity Points«.

A possible objection could be that this is not fair.

True - it is not as fair as the previously described alternative, where everyone must first earn their »Humanity Points«.

But it would not be as unfair as it first appears to be. Many rich people have earned their money legitimately (according to current social rules). The transfer of money from rich to poor is brought into motion with a motivating countervalue in form of »Humanity Points« and the money can be used more wisely for society. Sufficient money would significantly advance the introduction of »Humanity 10.0«.

There would be a further requirement in connection with the »Humanity 10.0« - values/rating system. A kind of conversion rate would be introduced; for yyy amount of money, you would get xxx amount of »Humanity Points«.

On the other hand, whether you should also get xxx »Humanity Points« for yyy amount of money should be carefully considered. »Humanity Points« would possibly become a kind of "second currency".

Exchanging »Humanity Points« into money would not be such a bad thing. Anyone working for the community acquires »Humanity Points«; these could then be exchanged into money to cover living costs, for example. It would be even better, if costs of living could directly be secured by »Humanity Points«.

If »Humanity Points« are provided with attractive benefits, such as exclusive services on the part of the society or important positions in organisations, they would be well worth striving for. Different conversion rates in the two exchange directions would provide an additional management tool.

A further interesting aspect of »Humanity 10.0« arises from the incorporation of all groups of people.

In addition to the healthy and able-bodied, there are also those who earn few (no) »Humanity Points«. They could still use their earned »Humanity Points«, but would somehow no longer be part of the system. There would be an interesting possibility of including this group. A simple example illustrates this point.

A person dependent on care is not able to earn »Humanity Points« for the social service "care". Society, family, or others will (hopefully) be able to care for this person. Those providing the "care" service get xxx »Humanity Points« for doing so because this is in the interest of the community.
What would happen if the person being cared for, could influence a certain number of »Humanity Points« for the service rendered to h m or her, i.e. "care"?
For example, a carer receives per patient and month 100 »Humanity Points«. If the person being cared for is happy with the service, the carer receives up to 10 further »Humanity Points«, if he or she is not happy, the carer receives up to 10 fewer points. Those who are not able to directly acquire »Humanity Points« for themselves could be considered as being influencers for the distribution of »Humanity Points«. Is that utopian?

Mechanisms that work in this way already exist. For example, it is possible to rate hospitals or doctors. Negative ratings mean fewer patients. In the long-run, economic survival would be at risk.
The greatest drawback of this kind of rating is that they are partly anonymous and have no consequences for those giving the ratings.

Currently and in future, a major challenge is ensuring the security of IT-Systems. Manipulation must be ruled out or be made extremely difficult. Security surrounding the mechanisms used for »Humanity 10.0« has the highest priority. »Humanity Points« may not arise without reason, they cannot get lost or be "rebooked".
It goes with-out saying that it must be possible to solve these technological challenges.
Aggressive attacks or manipulation of the values/rating system could be sanctioned by means of temporary or total exclusion.
New mechanisms would be made available through the

systematic and transparent rules of »Humanity 10.0«.
Furthermore, all groups of people can participate in shaping
»Humanity 10.0« and influence these rules.

What are further important contexts for »Humanity Points«?

A significant challenge will be to get inflexible social systems,
ideologies, religions, and all those who impose their systems
and ways of thinking onto others, on board. Since the existence
of
humanity, the all-encompassing "truth" has not been found and
this will not change. On the contrary - as soon as omniscient and
power-grabbing ways of thinking meet, major conflicts arise, often
leading to murder and manslaughter. This is precisely the reason
why »Humanity 10.0« has been designed as a flexible, neutral system. It is possible to compromise without "losing face" because of
an objective and impartial rating, based on actual issues.

A huge amount of challenges exist on earth and relate to all
people. We can only overcome these together and on a global
scale. At least for this purpose, a common approach must be
found. Thus, for the time being, the most important issues
worldwide would be subjected to rating by the »Humanity 10.0« -
values/rating system and other issues would gradually follow.

As you can see, the integration of the »Humanity 10.0« -
values/rating system is conceivable in many ways.
Who engages with »Humanity 10.0« and how, how many issues
are chosen for rating and how implementation should happen,
are still open points. This could develop differently, for example
in regions, countries or for groups of organisations.
If »Humanity Points« are convincing due to the positive effect
they have, they will ultimately prevail.

»Humanity 10.0« must be organised. The values/rating system
should function safely and destruction, as well as abuse must
be prevented. The existence of »Humanity 10.0« control mechanisms is incredibly important, in order to ensure its effectiveness
and continuous improvement. Furthermore, intelligent

management is also needed, so that conflict with what is already in place is kept to a minimum. However, this does not mean that a new and powerful organisation must be established. Necessary changes should still come about through the rating of issues and must be what we humans want.

For now, we will leave the extensive topic of installing »Humanity 10.0« in societies; further interesting aspects will be touched upon in Part 4. "Introducing »Humanity 10.0«.

In the next part 3 "How does »Humanity 10.0« operate?", we will initially look at some examples such as how best »Humanity 10.0« and the values/rating system can be effectively applied.

Part 3: How does »Humanity 10.0« operate?

Notes on the following examples

Optimal solutions for the future require the inclusion of as many framework conditions as possible – even those that are not readily talked about or we do not feel comfortable with.

In order not to give rise to any negative interpretations, the following is once again clarified; »Humanity 10.0« is intended for all people and supports the rights of people, that is human rights.

These human rights and much more unite us humans. We humans are still individuals and all different. This diversity has ensured our survival over millennia and is also considered by »Humanity 10.0«. However, the focus is on connecting people to each other.

In the following examples, the aim is to look at issues as objectively as possible and to initiate discussion on potential for improvement. It cannot be ruled out, that issues are connected to persons and organisations. Persons and organisations should not feel offended, but rather seize the opportunity to find a new niche.

One main objective of »Humanity 10.0« is to create incentives and promote achievements for the benefit of communities. Collaboration should be stimulated and strengths combined.

Fear is a strong motivation for us humans.
»Humanity 10.0« will certainly not motivate by using fear but one or the other issue can currently lead to fear.

Sanctions are not foreseen for the time being. Unfortunately, people have never managed without sanctions before. Sanctions can thus play a role during the development of »Humanity 10.0«. Possibilities for defence must be in place. Sanctions and defence are, however, not picked up on in the following examples.

In the following chapters some examples with diverse areas of focus will mainly show the different approaches to various issues and explain lines of thought.

Answers to any questions left open in connection with the following examples, can be found online at *www.humanity10.org* under *"Questions and Answers"*.

Example: Time constants

»Humanity 10.0« has a great potential in better adjusting the non-compatible time constants of widely varying issues. The potential results from the objective and logically comprehensible issues.

A short explanation follows, for all those who are not acquainted with time constants; as the name suggests, time is an observation quantity. The other quantity is the change in an issue. A time constant is a measure of how fast something can change/is changing.

A frequent problem is that the expected rate of change does not match the possible rate of change. This can be observed everywhere. An example is the expected progress of large construction projects which often did not correspond to what was realisable.
If everyone is aware of this and the difference between the expectations and the result is not too great, such an approach would not really be logical, but also not immediately detrimental. Unfortunately, there are many cases where this difference is quite considerable.

The example of "*high-frequency trading*" on the stock exchanges was already mentioned in Part 1. This is very well-suited example for illustrating the respective scheduled times and how extremely widely they can vary. Reminder: long-term developments of companies (months to years) are short-term assessments on the stock exchanges (milliseconds to hours). Criticism of high-frequency trading and proposals for change have been around for a long time. It is not an example specially construed for the purposes of »Humanity 10.0«. Let us look at some aspects.

During the coronavirus pandemic, people donated computing power to support research into combating the virus. Regardless of whether it made sense in this situation, people gave a clear signal, thereby indirectly expressing an expectation.
During the coronavirus pandemic, business on the stock exchange

simply continued as always, with very few restrictions and this although for many people, companies, and communities nothing was normal anymore. It may not have been a bad idea to also establish a kind of quarantine for the exchange. Switchable computing power for immediate crisis management would certainly be a sensible precaution for the future. In that case the stock exchange could be switched off and the computing power used elsewhere instead of happily continuing to be used for gambling on the stock market.

Just by thinking about it, it becomes obvious how dubiously some priorities have been set. In our first example the procedure of »Humanity 10.0« is shown, whereby the analysis and rating of issues via »Humanity 10.0« enables a better prioritisation. The changed approach illustrates the potential for improvement that can be found particularly in connection with (allegedly) "systematically relevant" issues.

There is no point in constantly assigning short-term assessments and actions to long-term developments. Our example clearly illustrates this inappropriate course of action because it is transparent and easy to understand.

First, let us recall the procedural steps per issue:

1. Stimulating reflection, initial assessments.
2. Collecting ideas for improvements.
3. Considering contexts.
4. *Using »Humanity 10.0« - areas of focus as rating criteria for the current status.*
5. *Using the rating criteria to assess the impact of known developments and ideas.*
6. Defining common goals and finding solutions.
7. Implementing idea(s) and monitoring progress.

Re. 1. Stimulating reflection, initial assessments

The facts:

- High-frequency trading generates rapid value changes in the millisecond range.
- Evaluations of large organisations, raw materials and much more are traded.
- Large organisations and raw materials etc. have very long development/change times.
- The short trading times do not match the long change times
- High-frequency trading requires a powerful infrastructure, particularly powerful computer performance with high energy consumption.
- The necessity of high-frequency trading is not comprehend-sible for normal human beings.
- The rapid changes in value endanger the financial system, as well as the rated organisations and developments.

Stimulating reflection and carrying out initial rating:

The pros of high-frequency trading are that:

- Investments have been made in technologies that are partially usable in other areas.
- ...

The cons of high-frequency trading are that:

- The trading speed does not correspond to the actual circumstances.
- Operating the trading platform ties up resources and consumes a lot of energy.
- No real value is created.
- There is no recognisable benefit for people.
- The computer capacity is not available to the general public

- The danger of stock market crashes increases, since it is hardly possible to intervene manually.
- ...

Based on this initial assessment, it is already clear that the cons overweigh the pros and that things must change.

Re. 2. Collecting ideas for improvements

Collecting ideas should initially be approached with an open mind. Ideas do not have to be fully developed during this phase.

Ideas regarding high-frequency trading could be as follows:

a) Make it even quicker;
b) Keep everything as it is;
c) Heavily tax it, making it unattractive;
d) Limit trading frequency;
e) Abolish it completely;
f) Change the entire financial system;
g) ...

Since everyone can contribute their ideas to »Humanity 10.0« non-objective proposals or those linked to specific interests will also be incorporated. The main effect during this phase will be that everyone who feels involved will have to engage and come up with suggestions. If those involved do not engage, ideas that are unfavourable for them could take shape.

Re. 3. Considering contexts

Since contexts can be very diverse, many issue ratings will have to be limited to the most important criteria.

Links to persons and organisations could play a role in connection with this step. These must be considered as part of reality.

How-ever, as little judgement as possible should be made about persons and organisations, since the focus is on the rating of the issue.

Facts and contexts can be best compiled with open questions, for example:

- How important is high frequency trade and what is it important for?
- Which added value (not only material) does high frequency trade have for societies?
- What would happen if high frequency trade would cease to exist?

The initial assessments made under 1. "Stimulating reflection, initial assessments" can be questioned once again. Also, contexts relating to the ideas collected in "Collecting ideas for improvements" in 2., could already play a role.

Re 4. Assessment of the current status

The »Humanity 10.0« areas of focus will be used as rating criteria for the current status.

*Assessment for the area of focus "**humanity as a whole**":*

Positive

- ...

Negative

- only a small part of humanity uses high-frequency trading,
- no added value, no recognisable benefit,
- part of a no longer transparent financial system,
- the financial system could even be destabilised,
- trading frequency too high compared to real developments,
- ...

High-frequency trading is of no great importance and partially contra-productive for the "whole of humanity".

*Assessment for the area of focus "**community**":*

Positive

- a small group profits from high-frequency trading,
- ...

Negative
- *groups of investors are disadvantaged,*
- *healthy companies/organisations can suffer damage,*
- *the reputation of the financial industry will be damaged,*
- *. .*

The high frequency trade has advantages for part of the "community". Many communities may suffer disadvantages.

*Assessment for the area of focus "**human**".*

Positive
- *Every person could benefit from the winnings gained,*
- *. .*

Negative
- *Alienation of the system from human activity,*
- *The ordinary person can profit little from it,*
- *...*

Although all people could participate, high-frequency trading is of little interest to the individual *"human"*.

*Assessment for the area of focus **"close surroundings"**.*

Positive
- *Expansion of modern infrastructure is financed and encouraged,*
- *...*

Negative
- *Strain on the energy and data infrastructures,*
- *...*

The importance of high-frequency trading for the "close surroundings" is only given if the necessary infrastructure is in the vicinity.

*Assessment for the area of focus **"entire environment"**:*

Positive
- *...*

<u>Negative</u>
- Computing capacity must be generated,
- Considerable energy consumption caused by high
  computing power,
- ...

High-frequency trading is harmful for the "entire environment" because of the resource and energy consumption.

A 3-level "quantitative rating" is illustrated in the following figure.

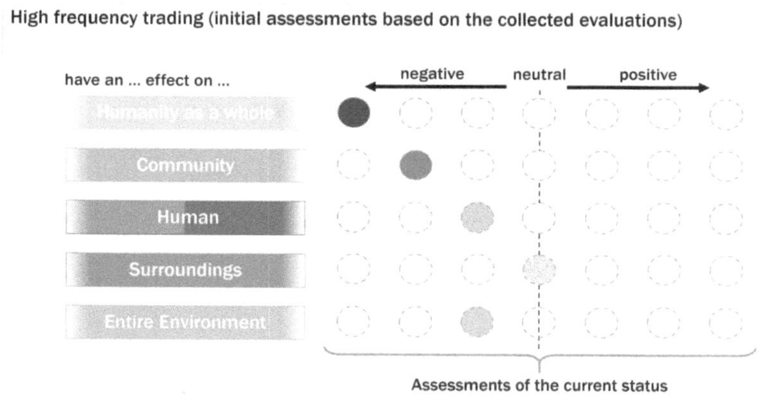

High frequency trading (initial assessments based on the collected evaluations)

Figure 7: High-frequency trading rating - current status

Re. 5. Assessing developments and ideas

High-frequency trading has been criticised for a long time. There have often been tentative attempts to improve the current situation, which fail regularly. The issue is not in the public focus. There are no prospects for improvement. Thus, there is no actual trend for change.
In cases such as these, it is appropriate to rate the ideas identified in step 2. This is what we want to do here.

The idea "completely abolish" will be slightly modified. This is necessary because changes, which are too drastic rarely make sense. Thus, the idea is amended and becomes a gradual abolition and after initial developments, the idea can be rated and, if necessary, modified again.

Since the procedure for the trends is like that of the assessment of the current status, i.e. the rating is carried out for the areas of focus "humanity as a whole", "community", "human", "close surroundings" and "entire environment", this will not be further specified again here.

The following summarised rating, results from the assessment of the mid- and long-term developments of the idea.

Assessment for the idea "stepwise withdrawal of high-frequency trading":

Positive
- *All negative aspects disappear entirely,*
- *Computing power can be used elsewhere,*
- *Resources can be used for beneficial things,*
- *Better equal opportunities for investors,*
- *Financial system has a less negative image,*
- *...*

Negative
- *Cost of the transformation of the financial system,*
- *...*

The idea to stepwise withdraw high-frequency trading has few disadvantages and many advantages.
The following figure illustrates the rating of the idea.

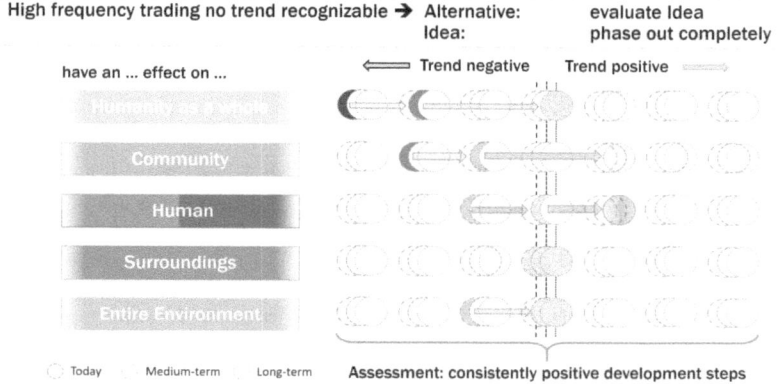

High frequency trading no trend recognizable ➔ Alternative: evaluate Idea
                                          Idea: phase out completely

Figure 8: Rating idea for high-frequency trading

As a result of the clear rating for high-frequency trading regarding the current status of known trends, as well as a potential idea, there is no need to conduct another detailed quantitative rating. High-frequency trading will not be able to receive any »Humanity Points«, but perhaps its abolishment will.

Re. 6. Defining common goals and finding solutions

How would solutions be found without »Humanity 10.0«? Stakeholder groups have probably not even introduced effective proposals in the idea phase to improve their negotiation position. In the solution-finding phase, each stakeholder group will work on its proposals again.

In this solution-finding step, care must be taken to ensure that the »Humanity 10.0« ratings are not questioned again. As soon as an idea is agreed on, the goal is clear and all those involved can work together to find solutions for implementation. Although »Humanity 10.0« is not about short-term successes, goals should be achievable within a reasonable amount of time.

Re. 7. Implementing idea(s) and monitoring progress

Implementing ideas and monitoring progress are standard practice in connection with »Humanity 10.0«.

Implementation itself is important, how it is monitored and by whom. In the case of the abolition of high-frequency trading, it is relatively easy because only the aspect of it being no longer in use needs to be monitored.

In Part 4 "Introducing »Humanity 10.0«", possible roles and responsibilities for the implementation of »Humanity 10.0« are described.

If advantages are to be made use of, for example switching computing power, then this is a separate process, involving additional planning and actions.

Concluding thoughts on the example "time constants"

The example of high-frequency trading is a good example of the effects it has, if time constants of trends do not match up with reality. It is surprising how well and for how long such obvious issues can be covered up. Perhaps, in the case of high-frequency trading, it has something to do with lobbying in connection with the financial system and that we humans are easily persuaded of potential necessities.

The subject "high-frequency trading" initially makes a global impression, only to be pushed into the "nationally unresolvable trend" category. However, in many cases, it is not about global or national. The will to change is lacking.
Thus, new ideas are called for.

Let us look at solutions presented to us by nature.

If a river is clogged
 (= solution obstructed),
 the

obstruction can be removed
 (=solution enforce)
  or
the water seeks a new path
 (= bypass solution)
  in

this way, the function is restored
 (= the system fulfils its purpose again).

Perhaps we think too seldom in "bypasses".

Why - if it obviously makes sense - not install a mechanism
which only allows trading of stocks once daily or weekly? All the
information on traded stocks is freely available to all and all the
respective rules transparent and easy to understand. Short selling
and other speculations are not allowed, or only to a limited extent.
The types of shares available could be limited to two.
In a new transparent trading system, shares are traded whereby
protection is provided against speculation and unnecessary price
fluctuations. In another trading system, speculation can continue
as before.

Would not the companies listed on the stock exchange and issuing
shares, perhaps even be interested in such a mechanism? There
are sufficient cases of companies that have left the stock exchange.
That would definitely benefit the ordinary investors, the people.

Mismatched time constants are common. Very positive changes
could be introduced here and quickly.

Example: We humans

Hav ng chosen high-frequency trading, we have looked at a global issue of great importance, that is not directly connected to persons or o ganisations.

The following example is an issue that can be looked at individually, is not of great importance, but is directly linked to persons. If individual processes of little significance occur frequently, they become more significant for humanity. The following example is about people and our actions.

Simple adjustments in our environment or in organisations and communities will not suffice to overcome the challenges ahead; we must change the way we think and act. As already indicated elsewhere in the book, we are not prepared to do this unless we have well-founded reasons.

Knowledge can sometimes be very helpful.
In school we have learned a lot about energy and power in physics classes. We can basically calculate how much energy is needed for what. We could even put different types of energy consumption in relation to each other. Why do we not use this knowledge?
We often regard this theoretical, memorised knowledge as pure information. We have been rewarded for it. Incorporating this knowledge into our daily lives was not a priority. There appears to be room for improvement here.

Facing interdependencies and consequences has never been and continues not to be popular. As described in the examples of the current status, this has not improved in the past years. We consume too much without thinking. For example, we consume too many resources and do not think about where they come from. We will regret this one day.

Let us look at the example **"gym"**.
To begin with, the facts; we want to stay fit and for this purpose, we go to the gym. There are several to choose from within a radius of 20 km, the closest being 3 km away; further gyms are

located 5 km, 10 km, 15 km, and 20 km away.

Our choice is made based on several individual preferences. Finally, we chose a gym, which is 10 km away. We use the car to get there, since our workout already uses up enough energy. Gyms located further away were not considered because the one that is 10 km away meets our expectations and the travel time would otherwise have been excessively long.

This example serves to reflect the way that most people think and act these days. The gym could just as well be a bakery or supermarket and the like.

The following interesting aspects arise, while looking at this straightforward case.

We are neither aware of the fact that we are moving our body with a car, which is ten times as heavy, nor is it of any avail. Most of the energy is not being utilised in our moving, but in that of the car. We will not question individual preferences, as these are important to us as a part of our overall satisfaction. Individual views vary quite considerably and this does not play a significant role in the case under consideration.

We instinctively reject any outside interference as an intrusion in our free space.

The environmental protection criterion has crept in because of the excessively long travel time, however it does not play a decisive role. If somebody, who is concerned about the environment asks us why we did not walk to the gym located 3 km away, we take great pains to explain why we do not (cannot) do that.

I apologise at this point to all those who have already declared environmental protection as their life principle.

That is the right attitude!

However, considering people on average, we are nowhere near to a sufficient measure of environmental protection. The current situation is sobering, as already determined at the beginning of the book.

Manipulating our genes, controlling us via chips in our bodies or brainwashing people to act rationally, are (hopefully) ruled out as possible solutions.

So, what now?

How could »Humanity 10.0« contribute?

To look at this, we use our steps again:

1. Stimulating reflection, initial assessments.
2. Collecting ideas for improvements.
3. Considering contexts.
4. ***»Humanity 10.0« - areas of focus as rating criteria for the current status.***
5. ***Using the rating criteria to assess the impact of known developments and issues.***
6. Defining common goals and finding solutions.
7. Implementing idea(s) and monitoring progress.

Re. 1. Stimulating reflection, initial assessments

We do not often think about changes voluntarily, we are far too stuck in the daily grind or do not have time - so we need an impulse. This impulse can be triggered by individual persons or communities. There is usually an influencer amongst friends and family. Environmental influencers are few and far between. These face a huge challenge in our consumption-oriented social environment.

The will of organisations could become an impulse.

It would be interesting to see what would happen if the gym were to only admit people who either came on foot or by bicycle and from a radius of 10 km. The gym would probably lose customers. Other customers would park their cars at a distance and just walk the rest of the way.

Government regulations could serve as an impulse.

However, these are often difficult to implement. The necessary checks can prove to be time-consuming and costly. People are constantly looking for loopholes, which must then be dealt with.

Refreshing our knowledge on physical interconnections would be an impulse, only can this have sufficient impact? The interconnections are clear. "The spirit is willing, but the flesh is weak"?

The impulse with the most impact is probably if most people change their tune und use their bicycles. For that to happen, biking and environmental protection would have to become trendy or something for everyone to strive for as a socially-acceptable standard.

We have now reflected on the case. With refreshed knowledge, it is clear to us, what makes sense.
Is this enough or do we need further impulses?
These could emerge, for example, if we look at further contexts.

The previous observations are also relevant for Part 4.
"Introducing »Humanity 10.0« ".

Re. 2. Collecting ideas for improvement

Ideas and suggestions can be helpful in showing that changes do not have to be something bad.

For our example, many options are possible:

- Going to the gym that is located 3 km away on foot or by bike;
- Always taking the bike to the gym;
- At least occasionally not using the car.

We do not always manage to change our behaviour radically. It is therefore helpful to introduce changes bit by bit and there are invariably ways and means of doing that.

Re. 3. Considering contexts

It does not always have to be the bigger picture; several smaller things can also be convincing.

If you are interested in cars or simply receptive to contexts, you create further links. Cars consume a disproportionally large amount of fuel during the first kilometres travelled.
A simple calculation leads to further insights. An economical car consumes roughly 5 litres/100 km, at first it consumes almost

double as much, that is 10 litres/100 km. For the gym located 10 km away, the round-trip amounts to 20 km in total. Thus, we use 2 litres of fuel for the journey to the gym; a litre of fuel currently costs approx. EUR 1.50.

The advantage of this context is that we humans can grasp the effect and we would be awarded in that we get a discount of EUR 3.00 for each visit to the gym.

The question is whether this suffices as an impulse?

Other contexts are more difficult for us humans to comprehend. If we convert the visit to the gym into an amount of CO_2, many people would register it, but it is not visible and they are not (yet) immediately affected by the imminent consequences.

How difficult it is to bring scientific knowledge and contexts to the attention of people over long periods of time has been demonstrated during the coronavirus crisis.

But we have also seen that based on their "swarm intelligence" or in the absence of their own findings, people follow scientific findings. The findings during the coronavirus pandemic were skilfully conveyed by use of targeted communication.

Considering contexts is essential and can generate additional insights. It is however necessary to package the resulting correct conclusions in an easily understandable way and to ensure a broad consensus.

Re. 4. Assessing the current status

The previous trains of thought were mainly related to us humans. Individual links to "environment CO_2" or rather "close surroundings" were established.

We now go over to assessing the trip to the gym by car according to the concept of »Humanity 10.0«.

Assessment for the area of focus *"humanity as a whole"*:

Positive

- ...

<u>Negative</u>
- ...

Going to a gym is of no (real) significance for "humanity as a whole".

Assessment for the area of focus **"community"**:

<u>Positive</u>
- *Community feeling will be strengthened by joint training sessions at the gym,*
- *Individual people's fitness also represents a value for society,*
- *...*

<u>Negative</u>
- *The exhaust fumes of the car are a nuisance for others,*
- *Parking places could be used more sensibly.*
- *...*

The visit to the gym has pros and cons for the "community". Although the disadvantages can be assigned to the journey with the car. The reasoning of supporting the car industry does not count because alternatives cannot develop in return.

Assessment for the area of focus **"human"**:

<u>Positive</u>
- *The car can protect in case of bad weather,*
- *Travel time is shorter by car,*
- *Travel by car is more comfortable,*
- *...*

<u>Negative</u>
- *Every trip with the car costs money,*
- *One's own health suffers because of exhaust fumes,*
- *Less physical activity,*
- *...*

Taking a trip to the gym has considerable advantages for people, the disadvantages only become clear after taking a second look. Compromises such as using the car in bad weather only could emerge.

Assessment for the area of focus **"close surroundings"**:

Positive
- *Streets will also be used by cyclists,*
- *Fewer emissions and less noise,*
- *...*

Negative
- *Costly infrastructure is necessary for the car,*
- *Direct damage to nature by emission,*
- *...*

The visit to the gym is strongly linked to "close surroundings" and this rating will thus have a substantial impact.

Assessment for the area of focus **"entire environment"**

Positive
- *...*

Negative
- *Every type of pollution damages our environment,*
- *...*

Travelling to the gym by car is harmful for the "entire environment". That said, it is the sum of the car journeys made by all people which have a significant impact, rather than the isolated case. The car journey dominates the issue, the gym is of minor importance. Somehow, the comfort of car travel does not really tally with the goal of getting fit.

Re. 5. Assessing developments and ideas

Some smaller trends can be identified in the case of the visit to the gym.

The energy consumption of the car will decrease. E-cars themselves no longer have any emissions in close surroundings. If electric energy is produced so that it is CO_2-neutral, the environment balance improves.

In the fitness sector, there could be a trend towards "home fitness", in which case the issue would be different.

Trends in personal behaviour are difficult to assess. It would be helpful at this stage to think through a few options for changes.

For example, these could be:
- To walk or cycle when the weather is nice and drive when it is not;
- To incorporate the arrival by bike as a "warm-up" to the fitness programme and departure as "cool-down";
- To combine the car journey to the gym with errands on the way.

If the importance of the issue is not so high, it is not necessary to analyse all details and trends. The advantages which evolve with each idea are often obvious.

Re. 6. Defining common goals and finding solutions

For issues in the private sphere, the behaviour of the individual is mainly decisive.
For joint solutions, it is necessary to form stakeholder groups. In our case carpooling to the gym would be such a common solution.

People who have worked on optimising their own personal ecological footprint have found that the individual's direct influence has limits. In these cases, we humans can and should demand the necessary changes. In our example, amendments in the case of local transport could be a solution to be organised socially, encouraged by those affected.

Re. 7. Implementing idea(s) and monitoring progress

In the personal sphere, ideas are almost always implemented by the individuals themselves. Monitoring potential progress will come down to the self-discipline of the individual.

Final thoughts on the example "gym"

Our life is (too?) diverse. Most decisions in the private sphere are (must be) made using "fast thinking" in order to stay on top of things. That is why we humans mostly need (simple) impulses for our thinking and acting, particularly when changes are to be initiated.

These impulses exist in different forms, but there is no one general impulse for all people. Since the general life situation of everyone is different and we react depending on the respecttive situation, individual impulses are often not enough.

Adjusting our behaviour again and again is important for ourselves. Most people as social beings will also change for the community. Change processes in the private sphere follow different principles to those of organisations, even if the issues and the goals are the same.

Example: Closing social bottlenecks

Social bottlenecks occur frequently in certain professions, as well as services. This can be a result of events, however there are also permanent bottlenecks. Taking a closer look at this shows that these problems rarely occur suddenly.

It is clear who contributes which value in a society. The think tank "nef" (new economics foundation) published a paper on this subject in 2009 "A Bit Rich: Calculating the real value to society of different professions".
It has been discovered that salaries in many professions do not tally with the share of value created in society, but little has changed so far. This mismatch, combined with the power of money is a major problem for societies. Why?

Many high performers in society improve their life as much as possible, which is quite understandable. Thus, they go for well-paid jobs. If professions without corresponding value creation are well-paid, high performers will migrate to these professions. Thus, they are lacking in other professions, which are important for society. So many high performers are not where they should be. Others want to be promoted to these financially lucrative positions. So, from a market economy perspective, there is large supply of applicants, yet salaries are still not reduced. The regulatory mechanism of supply and demand is not working as one would imagine. The reason for this could be that high performers are very competent and successfully defend their high rank. In this way the situation does not change.

Our next issue is the lack of carers in many countries, so let us address the practical example of *"care".*

Implementing the communal principle of solidarity in a transparent and ruthless manner would mean "anyone who has cared for somebody, has the right to be cared for". However, not everyone is able or suited to work in the care sector, although almost everyone can make another meaningful contribution to society.

To reduce the lack of carers by increasing pay seems the obvious thing to do. It is unclear, however, where the money will come from and whether more money will achieve the appreciation due. There are many people who have more money or earn more money daily, sometimes without providing the corresponding service to society.

With the use of the example "care", we want to show that, in particular, the »Humanity 10.0« - values/rating system can offer possible solutions.

As in the previous examples, we focus on the approach and implementation of the ratings using the steps:

1. Stimulating reflection, initial assessments.
2. Collecting ideas for improvements.
3. Considering contexts.
4. ***Using »Humanity 10.0«-areas of focus as rating criteria for the current status.***
5. ***Using the rating criteria to assess the impact of known developments and ideas.***
6. Defining common goals and find solutions.
7. Implementing idea(s) and monitoring progress.

Since the issue of "care" is relatively clear, what follows is only a summary of the ratings for our »Humanity 10.0« focus areas:

- Humanity as a whole;
- Community;
- Humans;
- Close surroundings; and
- The entire environment.

Re. "Humanity as a whole"

Not giving sufficient credit to activities of value to society is not a good thing for humanity as a whole. Migration of carers from one country to another (for reasons such as better pay) leads to dissonance between countries.

Re. "Community"

If a community was able to engage sufficient carers, there is initially no gap and therefore no need for this community to make any changes. Other communities, however have too few carers. For »Humanity 10.0«, the average demand of all communities is decisive. The result is an unmet need, presumably due to underpayment.

Re. "Humans"

In the case of the area of focus "humans", the circumstances are no other than those of the "community".
There will be people who are not affected, many are provided for, others not. On average, there are too few carers and this can become a problem for each individual person.

Re. "Close surroundings"

Care is not directly connected to close surroundings. However, the migration of carers can cause an environmental impact, for example as a result of traffic.

Re. "The entire environment"

The shortage of carers is not an environmental problem. If there are no new insights, this focus area would be set to "neutral = cannot be assessed".

As can be seen, the »Humanity 10.0« rating turned out to be what was basically already expected. There are too few carers, presumably because this occupation is not sufficiently appreciated. This must be changed.

Ideas for solutions could be the following:

- More advertising for the profession;
- Arousing public interest;
- Better pay;
- Higher social appreciation.

Important for us is to sort out how »Humanity 10.0« can contribute?

Let us recollect one of the »Humanity 10.0« principles "thinking in the original position – anything can happen to anyone". The issue "care" would be more strongly supported because anyone can be affected by it. This is basically clear, it is, however, often forgotten. Thus »Humanity 10.0« raises more public awareness of the issue and appreciates its importance. It may be that this results in better pay. »Humanity 10.0« is, however, unable to bring money into circulation or to redistribute it.

Let us consider »Humanity Points«, in this way there is certainly the possibility of valuing carers more. After all, important services to society would all be rewarded with »Humanity Points«. In a fully established »Humanity 10.0« - values/rating system, »Humanity Points« would not only have an appreciative value. Everyone could use the »Humanity Points« for services provided by society. This simple and coherent solution would motivate people to champion nursing professions and take a greater interest in the common good.

The described issue "caring" is a prime example for many other professions and services, that people provide for society.
The coronavirus pandemic brought important services more into focus for us humans. Applause to show gratitude is important for the time being. However, even more important is to look to the future and reflect about an appropriate way of showing appreciation, as well as questioning our societal priorities.

According to current mechanisms, all disadvantaged (or those who fee disadvantaged) groups could (and do) strike. An opportunity such as this to express one's will, is an important part of democracy. But every strike drains energy from a society.
Thus, all other possibilities to eliminate social discrepancies should be taken advantage of first.

With its values/rating system, »Humanity 10.0« offers a future-oriented approach for fairer appreciation and rewarding of services rendered. Since we humans can determine for ourselves what is of value for us, real improvements would be possible for societies.

Example: Social qualifications

In the past and even nowadays, people can assert themselves in managerial positions, despite not being eligible. This hardly plays a role at lower management levels. However, even mid-level managers must work with larger groups of people and may have to make serious decisions, which affect big communities. Thus, it is of essential importance that the right leaders are selected for communities, as well as for societies as a whole.

Let us look at the current situation in the world.
There are extreme situations, where, figuratively speaking "sheep are ruled by a pack of wolves". It is clear what goes on in such a scenario. This makes no sense for the community, the "sheep". Everyone can imagine where this problem occurs, perhaps in not such an extreme form.

One thing is clear: Every potential leader should / must be able to demonstrate a certain level of commitment to communities.
Is this currently happening to the extent that it should be?
The necessary foundations for a qualified selection according to the criteria for social competence are in place. However, these are not easy to apply and ultimately the body responsible for making the selection prioritises their use.

In our next example **"key official positions"** we look at which contribution »Humanity 10.0« can make, particularly the intro-duction of »Humanity Points«.
To be able to better illustrate this example, we chose the leadership role of "chief" of a tribe.

The leadership functions include:

- Ensuring the existence of the tribe;
- Cooperating with other "leaders";
- Organising peaceful coexistence;
- Defending the tribe against attacks, if necessary;
- Being a positive example for others;

- "Taking care" of the community;

How well do the current "chiefs" fulfil these leadership tasks? That certainly depends on many marginal conditions, particularly the size of the community. If we are not satisfied with the leadership, this could be because the current selection criteria do not meet the requirements.

It would be so important for captains to be in control of their ship, to know their properly selected crew well and to achieve a high level of safety and satisfaction for the passengers. Should this not be the case, perhaps the next iceberg is looming on the horizon for all concerned.

At this point, we will not go into current situations any further, but rather establish the link to »Humanity 10.0«.

The value of the issue of filling key positions appropriately is indisputable. Using »Humanity 10.0« criteria for issues and thus for "governing" is not the decisive point in our example. We want to see which impact the use of »Humanity Points« can have. The idea is, that each "chief" requires »Humanity Points« to be able to assume office.

In the run-up to selection, the "chief" will always be confronted with five questions.

Is what he does (issues), positive or negative for:

- All tribes (humanity as a whole);
- His tribe (community);
- Each person in his tribe (human);
- The territory of the tribe (close surroundings);
- Everything on earth (the entire environment).

The potential "chief" receives »Humanity Points« for positive actions and points are deducted for negative actions.
Presumably there are further candidates for the position of "chief". These candidates are subject to the same ratings.
The ratings are related to the issues, the »Humanity Points« and

are set in advance. There are no personal preferences, that is, no personal influences that change the rating of the issues. The potential "chiefs" will therefore have to align their performance for the people and environment to positive criteria, in order to accrue enough »Humanity Points«.

The following positive effects result:

- Values are created for all;
- Selection criteria are transparent for all;
- Unsuitable candidates will not be able to fulfil the criteria in the long run;
- This serves as practise for the skills needed for later leadership;
- Those who always stick to the rules, will not break them so easily later.

For wrongly "acquired" »Humanity Points«, sanctions are conceivable or exclusion from the election for "chief". Regarding the election, there is nothing preventing a final election by the tribe, the people. The values/rating system provides transparent decision criteria but they do not have to be final.

For that example, it is not a condition that the »Humanity Points« are completely introduced and on a compulsory basis. A voluntary system for individual items would also function. That means that whoever voluntarily collects as many »Humanity Points« as possible over time, would have an advantage at the election

In case one or the other leader still does not do everything right and breaks out in a sweat when reading this example, a short note to reassure – everyone can continually improve!

»Humanity Points« will probably only be available in xx years. From that point on they can be accrued by everyone.
For the socially important jobs, a minimum of »Humanity Points« will be necessary. Thus, the appropriate posts would even be socially upgraded.

Currently, no leaders would lose their positions due to the introduction of »Humanity 10.0«.
However, (still) more engagement for people and environment or orientation towards the »Humanity 10.0« criteria, would be a very good idea.

Example: Avoiding the "unnecessary"

In the next example, »Humanity 10.0« is used to tackle another challenge. The focus is on how to avoid the "unnecessary". Only, what is unnecessary?

To better understand the issue, we look at the subject of **"unnecessary products".**

What are unnecessary products?
Opinions can differ on this question. The following definition, could however fit; unnecessary products are things that can be dispensed with without further ado. Such products are mostly purchased because an artificial need is generated as a result of targeted marketing. During the last decades, people have been conditioned to consume. It is not easy to change this state of conditioning. Unnecessary products are those which are unusable after a short time, that is, poor quality items, or rather those with a short service life.

The market regulates that the unnecessary or low-quality products are no longer in demand after a while. This is often, but not always, the case.
The manufacture of unnecessary products consumes resources. These resources, such as oxygen and water, belong to us all. It would therefore be justified for us to decide - even before production - whether the resources should be used for such unnecessary products, since these resources are then lacking for worthwhile causes.
If an unnecessary product is not produced, we save 100% of resources.

It is not necessary to reinforce this with the »Humanity 10.0« criteria. However, we want to consider some common arguments.

A widely used line of argumentation is:

$\Rightarrow$ Fewer products;
$\Rightarrow$ Lower turnover;

⇒ Lower economic output;

⇒ Job losses;

⇒ Reduction in prosperity.

This line of argumentation is, however simply wrong. Neither the number nor the variety of products necessarily has an impact on sales. The same turnover can also be generated with higher-quality products.
Economic output is an artificial definition that reveals nothing about the usefulness of the actual output.
The production of unnecessary products does not protect against job losses and does not reduce prosperity.

Another line of argument is also dubious; the cheap products exist so that as many people as possible have access to them. Conversely, this means that those who cannot afford good, expensive products, should, at least buy those with a low value in use. In purely arithmetical terms, many unnecessary products add up to one better, more useful product. Having to buy a product again because of the poor quality, can make it even more expensive.

Meanwhile products must meet considerable environmental standards. That is very good. An unnecessarily item produced to these same high standards, is still harmful to the environment. It has no worth and has, as a result of its production, burdened the environment.

Who now thinks that the production of creative and varied products is no longer allowed, is wrong. It is simply a fact that there are many regulations about all sorts of things around products. Whether or not it makes sense is something that the companies are free to consider. Why should we not support these deliberations more?
For many people, it is probably easier, to choose from 20 different products than from 100.

Even if only 5% of the unnecessary products are no longer produced, 5% of resources would be saved without our assistance. That is excellent; we purchase 5% fewer, presumably dispensable, products and can simultaneously save money and do something for the environment.

"Unnecessary products" are not unnecessary if they give pleasure. Art, culture, collecting things and making useful purchases makes sense. »Humanity 10.0« wants us humans to see a purpose in our lives and be satisfied. Does mass consumption or wanting unnecessary possessions make sense and really make us happy? Everybody must decide that for themselves.

Since there is no unlimited growth, changes are inevitable in the next decades. It does therefore make sense to forgo what we do not need anyway.

Whoever cannot survive without mass consumption, will have to look for a new purpose in life, at the latest, in a few years' time.

Until now, this example has had no real »Humanity 10.0«-specific connection. »Humanity 10.0« could provide further arguments as to why we should no longer buy unnecessary, poor quality products or those with a short lifespan.

»Humanity 10.0« comes into its own elsewhere; it serves to offer an alternative sense of purpose, or rather satisfaction.

Those who stand up for people and the environment are rewarded with »Humanity Points«. A point system which functions in the opposite direction than so far, i.e. collecting discount points for sales made: In this case those who buy nothing get points.

That would make sense and can also lead to satisfaction.

Summary for the examples

Issues can be sufficiently well-rated with the criteria of the values/rating system of »Humanity 10.0«, that means, whether they are valuable for us humans, whether improvements should be made or whether they are no longer necessary.

Even without carrying out all the steps and an exact quantification, the issues can be assessed so well that priorities can be redefined.

In order to be able to meet the upcoming challenges, we need resources on all levels. In many cases, these resources are tied up in issues with dubious benefit. Resources for necessary changes would, in principle, be available, but we must really try to rid ourselves of unnecessary issues and not just talk about them. »Humanity 10.0« could help with this.

As can be seen in the various examples, Humanity 10.0« can provide benefits during the different steps. Some of these benefits can be used individually.

It is not necessary to apply the »Humanity 10.0« - values/rating system, with all its possibilities for all issues. Just qualitative ratings of the most important issues using the criteria of »Humanity 10.0« would have a gigantic benefit.

Further advantages of »Humanity 10.0« can be found in Part 5 "Motivation", in the chapter "Advantages for…".

Part 4: Introducing »Humanity 10.0«

Basic considerations

After becoming acquainted with »Humanity 10.0« in the previous chapters, the question now arises: "How can »Humanity 10.0« be introduced?" What good is the best idea if we do not know how to implement it.

»Humanity 10.0« is straightforward with its 5 simple questions on the areas of focus. However, since the system can be applied to almost any issue, it results in an enormous diversity. Using »Humanity 10.0« to support global changes is an additional challenge.

Much is discussed in circles of friends, groups of regulars, meetings in pubs and clubs, religious communities, parties, scientific forums, and many other places where people get together. Many of these places serve to entertain, others to strengthen the sense of community or to develop ideas. People often agree on conclusions arising from these discussions and on the fact that some things must change. Even the one or other good idea arises. What is more difficult, is turning these ideas into actions.

In the chapter "Principles", the two fundamentally different ways of thinking "fast thinking" and slow thinking", were mentioned. We are comfortable in our ways – even when we think, we are quick to agree to an idea, however, we find it difficult to systematically follow this through, particularly in the face of possible resistance. Is that a bad thing? No, but it is a pity.

We must consider that most people will not actively participate in the development of »Humanity 10.0« and many people will not change their behaviour without sufficient impulses or pressure. People will, however, support things that make sense. Thus, for the introduction of »Humanity 10.0«, we need a plan, which is closely aligned to the possibilities of realising ideas.

Requirements for the introduction

To be able to install »Humanity 10.0« according to the described characteristics, a targeted introduction is important.
The introduction of »Humanity 10.0« should take place in the following manner:

Openly:

- Participation of all people, communities, and organisations
    ⇒ objective, impartial movement

Flexibly:

- Implementation and design
    ⇒ per country, per groups of countries, globally
    ⇒ per group of persons/organisations

In a communicative manner:

- Using all communication channels
- Collecting and evaluating progressive ideas
- Enabling discussions/ratings

Reliably:

- Protecting personal data and sources
- Using secure information

Multilingually:

- Translation into as many languages as possible

Introductory steps

The following steps to introduce »Humanity 10.0« are planned:

1. Publish idea and plan.
2. Refine concept.
3. Create »Humanity 10.0«-platform.
4. Promote the idea
   a) Advertising the idea
   b) Targeted search for sponsors.
5. Further expand the movement.
6. »Humanity 10.0«-pilot applications.
7. Develop values/rating system(s).
   a) Evaluate information/experiences.
   b) Create »Humanity Points«.
8. Use values/rating system(s).

Re. 1. Publish idea and plan

In the first phase, publications in German, English and French language versions are planned:

- Internet presence: *www.menschheit10.org*;
  www.humanity10.org;
  www.humanite10.org
- Flyer (1-page and 4-page);
- Presentations (Overview, examples);
- Questions and answers;
- Wikipedia entry;
- Book: "Menschheit 10.0"
  "Humanity 10.0"
  "Humanite 10.0"

Translations in as many languages as possible are planned; when these will be available is not clear.

Re. 2. Refine concept

»Humanity 10.0« is a very large project. All the details can only emerge bit by bit. The current concept is constantly being questioned and improved. For the launch, the areas of focus will be determined and issues chosen, depending on how many and which partners participate.
In order to be able to advance a topic, a basis must exist. »Humanity 10.0«, as a concept is a basis for discussion. Some parts are coherent and can be realised, others still require input.

Re. 3. Create »Humanity 10.0« - platform

Collaboration on »Humanity 10.0« must be organised. A platform must be created, which enables distribution of information and widespread communication.

The following points are important for organising collaboration:

- Establish strategy and rules;
- Describe type and scope of tasks;
- Recruit the necessary skills;
- Define necessary steps;
- Establish a "starting organisation".

A core team, that can organise the further steps for introduction, must be established. Everyone can get involved in »Humanity 10.0« in different ways. Whoever is interested in actively participating, should visit: *www.humanity10.org* or alternatively, write an email to *info@humanity10.org*.

The first 3 steps to introduction are not yet very specific. In the following steps, the coordination between the structure of »Humanity 10.0« and the planned introduction will become clearer.

Re. 4. Promote the idea

In today's day and age, it is not easy to place a new idea in such a way that it is really visible in the vast amount of information out there. Even spectacular actions sometimes get lost in the mass.

How long did Greta Thunberg have to sit there, for example, before she was noticed and her concern for environmental protection affecting us all was heeded.

Let us imagine that a normal adult sits in front of the parliament or any other public place. Whatever is written on that person's sign, it would probably not be perceived as a serious representative of an idea. The person may be pitied or measured up in some other social context. Individual actions do not achieve the effects necessary for the establishment of »Humanity 10.0«.

That is why the following activities are envisaged, in order to plant the idea in people's heads bit by bit.

Advertising the idea

These days symbols or "brands" are often the way to gain visibility and success. This ensures that identification with the basic idea can come about, without having to follow the details of each development.

The symbol/brand »Humanity 10.0« would be a non-profit brand. It is not about making profit with the brand but to create a distinguishing feature.

It takes time and professional marketing to develop a symbol / brand and ensure sufficient public visibility.

Targeting potential interested parties

It is easy to ignore what is going on around us.

It is something quite different to be approached about certain issues and to have things – so to speak – thrust at you. With today's sensory overload, even if someone is addressed, a reaction is, unfortunately not guaranteed. The method of addressing is thus targeted and transparent. People will be interested in who reacted and how.

In the case of »Humanity 10.0«, everyone should be involved, which is why the type and extent of those to be addressed is not limited. It makes sense to start with "promising" people and organisations.

Why is the focus on the aspects "brand" and "addressing" for the introduction of »Humanity 10.0«?

There are already many progressive organisations with outstanding achievements for communities. Many have their own and some even similar symbols/brands, for example "...for Future" or "... 4 Future". Why a separate brand for »Humanity 10.0«?

As already indicated at the beginning of the book, these progresssive initiatives mostly have a single focus and no overall approach for the comprehensive reorientation of the very diverse communities / societies. Many of the initiatives work on the improvement of current situations, some have a medium-term focus. However, they will all have to work together in future, in order to meet the upcoming challenges.

In this context, imagine that an initiative would try to gain the upper hand. Or in other words, one symbol/brand would dominate, others would be less visible or "taken over".

»Humanity 10.0«, on the other hand, wants to preserve diversity. Those who are already involved in society, can continue doing just that. All initiatives can continue to further develop their identity, including symbols/brands.

Another argument for a new symbol/a new brand is that this can still be fleshed out as desired, in terms of content.

There are no inherited burdens or predefined content and no restrictions on thinking and acting. In the case of »Humanity 10.0«, issues should be able to be dealt with as freely as possible without any encumbrances.

There is also a further argument. Many people do not engage, although several innovative initiatives have been around for some time. Perhaps these people are more interested in a strategic initiative, such as »Humanity 10.0«.

»Humanity 10.0« wants to integrate and achieve goal-oriented cocperation across seemingly invincible barriers.

Which organisation(s) would currently be able to do this?

A further implementation focus is: »Humanity 10.0« should be designed as a flexible, future-proof system, which is not vulnerable. Dismissing the 5 simple questions regarding the usefulness of an issue (for us humans, communities, humanity, close surroundings, and the entire environment) as being pointless, is not so easy.

The values/rating system will be developed together by all of us. Whoever is involved from the very beginning, has an immediate influence on its design.

When the values/rating system is eventually installed, all those who have contributed to the community, as well as those who have been involved in the development of »Humanity 10.0«, could receive »Humanity Points«. Based on the above, targeting individuals and organisations seems to be a promising way forward.

Many organisations already have a progressive programme. For some, these are initially only declarations of intent, but targeted inquiries could advance implementation.

In Part 5, "Motivation", the benefits of »Humanity 10.0« for various groups of people and organisations are described. When addressing them, these benefits would be referred to.

To get a better impression of who should be addressed, here are a few examples:

- Organisations, for example "…for Future", …
- Universities, Institutes, …
- Scientists, artists, influencers, …
- UN, EU, governments, …
- Media, for example TV, press, internet.

Addressing these groups should consider the current positions of the people and organisations.
This will be discussed in more detail in the next point.

Re. 5. Further expanding the movement

Addressing persons, groups of persons and organisations occurs with the aim of generating widespread support for the idea. For that purpose, every possible type of support is welcome, for example liking the idea, spreading the idea, following the idea, actively collaborating, providing services, donating and so on.

»Humanity 10.0« will need many active supporters. These should be people and organisations who see the necessity for comprehensive changes and would like to become involved.

If »Humanity 10.0« is supported by large or important organisations, this will result in considerably improved framework conditions. Major projects can be implemented with the help of professional support.

Support by all existing progressive initiatives, people and organisations would be ideal. It is not a matter of people moving from one initiative to another, but of mutual benefit, that is progressive forces and »Humanity 10.0« supporting each other.

Existing structures are very valuable and a good and quicker way of moving forward.

»Humanity 10.0« also wants to encourage communities, people and organizations that have not been particularly progressive so far to take the opportunity and become involved in certain topics, or rather »Humanity 10.0«.

The conflicts between states, do not emanate from people but are fuelled by governments, individual groups, or even just individual leaders. Sometimes, however, only a kind of "stalemate" occurs in which any kind of acquiescence in form of "weakness" does not seem to be an option.

Religions sometimes share common values. It is therefore more than astonishing that religious conflicts occur.

If these circumstances are questioned by us humans via »Humanity 10.0« then perhaps this could prompt the respective communities and organisations to act.

Why should there not be initiatives such as:

- Governments for humanity;
- Religions for humanity;
- …

The "House of Humanity" designed by us humans has many pillars. The pillars stand on a common foundation, the environment. »Humanity 10.0« as a connecting element for better stability of the pillars and at the same time as "protection against negative influences" – would that not be a nice idea?

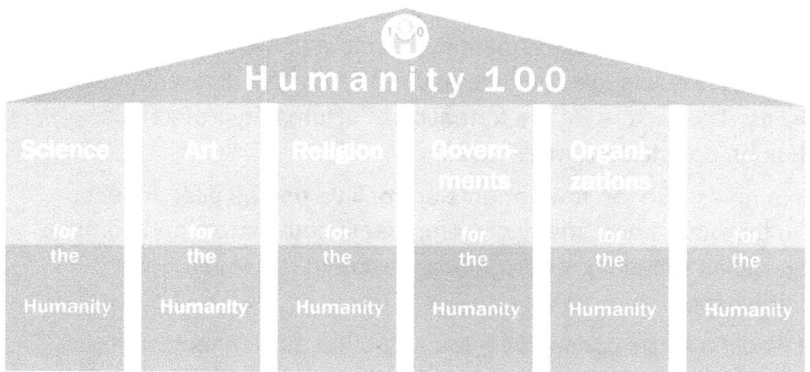

Figure 9: The House of Humanity

Re. 6. »Humanity 10.0«-pilot applications

The procedure per issue has already been described and illustrated with the help of initial examples. The introduction, or rather the test to see how the ratings work, as well as the attempt to award »Humanity Points« should be carried out by means of many "pilot projects".
Existing scientific know-how as well as all the experience from the already installed "stand-alone solutions" should be incorporated into these projects. In this way, further ideas can be generated for the values/rating system.

Which issues are suitable as pilot projects?

One option would be to expand on existing rating systems and enhance them, using the »Humanity 10.0« criteria. In case the existing rating criteria already have a comparable focus, quantification could be the next step, that is to go over to generating »Humanity Points«.

A high level of acceptance could be achieved if the most urgent challenges were considered first and thus initial implementation would be possible immediately after the pilot phase.

Making a systematic selection of issues would help to quickly convert the value/assessment system to a universal status. In this way, knowledge could be gathered from the different subject areas. The factors for the formation of »Humanity Points« can thus be coordinated more quickly.

Examples with too few variants are of little use as pilot projects. On the other hand, many diverse, that is both simple and complex examples with sufficient significance, could result in a good combination.

It would also be conceivable to carry out a quick check on many issues with the »Humanity 10.0« rating criteria, in order to generate a reasonable selection for more detailed rating.

Precisely this approach of "rating issues quickly by means of the 5 questions" would be suitable for each individual. The questions of whether the issue is positive or negative for humanity as a whole, the community, humans, close surroundings, and the entire environment would indicate potential for improvement. If the questions are asked consistently of many issues, new meaningful priorities arise.

Re. 7. Develop values/rating system(s)

First suggestions for the »Humanity 10.0« - values/rating system have already been described; there were ideas for its structure, further developments, and the introduction. In the following a brief summary will be given.

Rating all the very different issues in connection with the areas of focus,

- Humanity as a whole;
- Community;
- Humans;

- Close surroundings; and
- Entire environment,

is quickly applicable as a basic idea.

The first assessments already show, which issue is rated positively and which negatively. The next step is the quantitative rating, as well as the addition of the trends to the issue.
After that, the correlations between the issues and the areas of focus must still be rated, so that a coordinated rating system is established. When everything comes together, the »Humanity Points« can be brought in.

In the previous steps, ratings are aimed at, which concentrate exclusively on the issues.
A link to persons and organisations first takes place in the next step. At this point, the value of »Humanity Points« must already be clear and how they will be integrated into our lives.
A part of that is the incentive, which only arises when appropriate countervalues are provided for the »Humanity Points«. Ideas and suggestions are particularly needed at this point. The more attractive the countervalues for »Humanity Points« are, the quicker and more effective the values/rating system can be implemented.

Designing the values/rating system and defining logical »Humanity Points« will be fascinating tasks related to »Humanity 10.0«.
At that point, as many people as possible should be interested in »Humanity 10.0«.

Re. 8. Use values/rating system(s)

The future will tell what status that »Humanity 10.0« and its values/rating system will have one day. The chances are good, however, that »Humanity 10.0« will be installed (or something comparable under a different name).
There are many benefits!

Is there a better solution than the introduction of a new flexible "currency" system, linked to human values and real value creation?

What would be the alternatives?

Like constantly trying to improve existing societies with individual incentives and "minimal reforms" and merely trying to prevent the worst?

We do not have the time of several generations; we must take future-oriented action now.

Who implements »Humanity 10.0« and how?

The described steps for the introduction of von »Humanity 10.0« are of a fundamental nature. However, an introduction takes place in the current societal environment and not "on the greenfield".
In order to be able to adapt the introduction scenarios to the current conditions, it is necessary to take a closer look at them.

As a neutral movement, the »Humanity 10.0« organisation is not equipped to be able to fully implement a values/rating system and does not endeavour to be in that position. This means that existing governmental and societal structures will play an   important role, especially in its implementation.

There are many – some vary varied - societal structures around the world, for example:

- European Union;
- USA;
- Russia;
- China;
- Religiously-ruled countries;
- Developing countries;
- Underdeveloped countries;
- … areas isolated from civilization.

If and how well »Humanity 10.0« can position itself in these structures is pure speculation.
We should concentrate on furnishing »Humanity 10.0« with so many benefits, that it becomes widely accepted amongst people and there is no way around its being introduced.

Thus, some important benefits for the introduction as follows:

»Humanity 10.0« will be developed in parallel to everything that already exists

- Long-term, systematic development of a new and sustainable system;
- Widespread participation of everyone in societies;
- Positive outlook generated for us humans;
- Differences in societies are not knock-out criteria;
- Current experiences and tools from different areas can be used.

The introduction can be arranged flexibly

- Areas of focus deliberately selectable (priority and time);
- Impact on individuals and organisations controllable per issue;
- No compulsory standard for everything, for example, free choice of the issues according to relevant needs.

The advantages of flexibility should not, however, lead to other asp red principles or values having to be abandoned.
The system, or rather, the structures, should not become too con⁻using or complex.

What follows, is a proposal for the organisational and structural introduction.

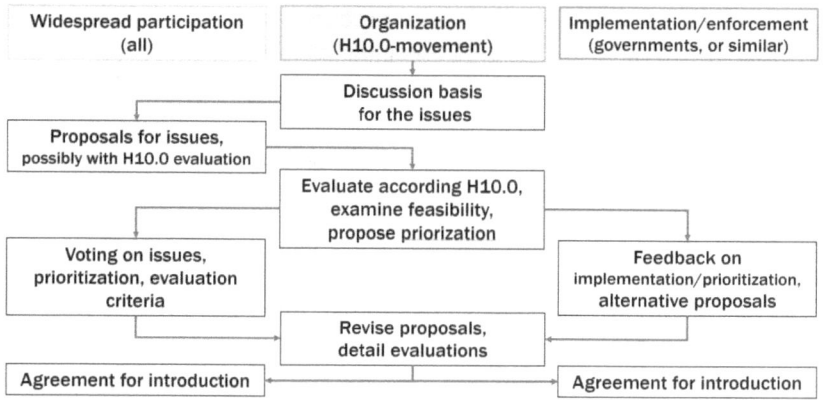

Figure 10: Proposal for the introduction structure

Let us first look at the three top boxes of stakeholder groups.

"Widespread participation (all)" means just that; all people, communities, and organisations – really anyone at all - can participate.

"Organisation (»M10.0«-movement)" stands for the movement of all those interested in »Humanity 10.0«, from a wide variety of fields. Widespread cooperation is aimed at. Each person or organisation decides, if they want to actively participate in the development of »Humanity 10.0« and thus also incorporate their interests.
The decisive aspect of this movement is that due to the diversity of the participants, an "average neutrality" ensues and nobody can dominate the movement. Decisions should be made based solely on objective rating of issues.

»Humanity 10.0« also requires an actual organisation. This has the task of creating all the necessary organisational requisites, in-stalling, and monitoring processes and bringing about decisions. The neutrality and integrity of this organisation are crucial for wide-spread acceptance. Any links to organisations must not have a decisive influence on substantial decisions.

"Implementation/enforcement (governments)" clarifies, that the »Humanity 10.0« organisation sees itself as an intermediary between people's ideas and values and the governments and organisations responsible for implementation. The existing social structures are to be used for implementation and enforcement.

Furthermore, there are higher level, influential organisations, such as the United Nations, religious communities, and large corporations. It would not make sense to ignore the interdependencies prevailing in many countries between governmental and non-governmental organisations. This means that parts of the implementation would also take place through these organisations.

Since concentrations of power could arise in the area of implementtation and enforcement, the movement of »Humanity 10.0« will still have a control function. It is necessary to look at what the broad mass of people and societies want and enforce this. Apart from that, the rating cycles for issues must be planned and monitored, as well as potential improvements collected.

How the registration of the potential and the organisation of the ratings should be secured, is illustrated in the following figure.

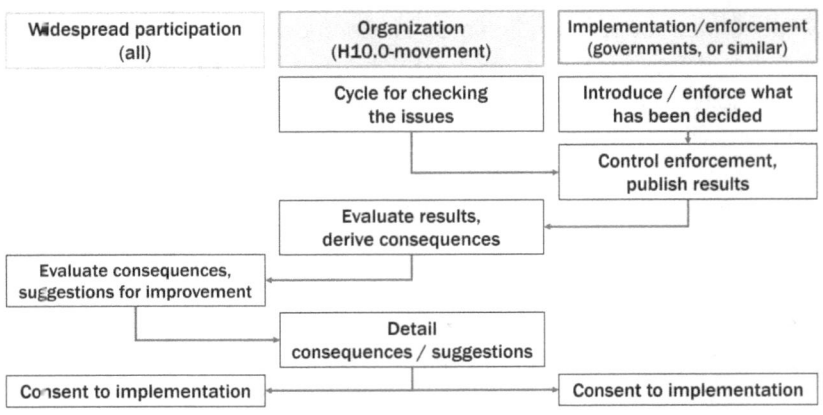

Figure 11: Suggestion for ensuring success

People express their priorities and effectively get these monitored. In addition, decisions made are regularly questioned, and if necessary, corrected.

Such approaches to "grassroots democracy" have always existed and occur every now and again. Why have they not been able to gain acceptance so far?

One reason could be that "grassroots democracy" was and is too strongly linked to the "power question".

If they are satisfied, most people don't care how and by whom they are governed. They are content if they can express their wishes and a part of these are fulfilled. They are not unhappy if the wishes are not implemented for plausible reasons, or if alternative solutions are available.

However, people are seldom asked what they want. On the contrary, it is suggested to them from many sides, what they should want.

For many people, it would perhaps be more important to always receive help in the event of illness in a health care system, which is not a high-profit company focused on getting the maximal usage from all the functions of technical gadgets. The developer of the various functions may even prefer that his or her idea has the greatest possible value for people. And no – the market does not regulate it. There are too many influential organisations with their own interests for that to happen.

Questions essential for us humans are far too seldom asked. Instead people are bombarded with vast amounts of products, information, sensations and much more, until they are inundated with stimuli and submissive – not even enjoying the hundredth piece of clothing – losing their human identity more and more while typing away on their cell phones. This is then described as being progress.

Another situation is also no better.
In this case, it is conveyed to us humans that the "philosopher's stone" has already been found and that the world functions

"thus and only thus". Every human should be guided by this way of thinking and then everything is / will be good.

Others doubt the human will or the existence of self-determined humans altogether.

Everyone can / should form their own opinion as to where these modes of thought lead to.

From the point of view of »Humanity 10.0«, there are three implementation messages to the different social structures:

1. Those, who decide to embody progress, should quickly develop new, progressive ideas.
2. All those who are not open to new opinions and ideas, will never achieve what is best for the people, no matter what they say.
3. A request to the others, help both to find a new way of thinking, but do not, under any circumstances, adopt the opinions of 1. or 2.

Going back to the "grassroots democracy", this functions on a small scale in many cases - however, not yet on a large scale. With »Humanity 10.0«, new general conditions arise for the introduction and use of "grassroots democracy". It is about opinions based on issues and decisions for the benefit of people and the environment. A system arises from the total of the individual issues, made up of objective wishes and the possibility to be able to realise those wishes better with the help of an incentive scheme (»Humanity 10.0« - values/rating system).

When introducing »Humanity 10.0«, we must consider all the very different ways of thinking and expectations that people have. »Humanity 10.0« is about the development of a sustainable system for the future and not about spontaneous unrealistic dreams, however these came about.

"Fast thinking" can be a good way of supplying ideas and help in assessing their effect on us humans. The actual development of »Humanity 10.0« must be dealt with by means of the strenuous "slow thinking" and with scientific precision.

For both ways of thinking, as well as the entire introduction, the positive result is ultimately decisive.

How quickly can and should »Humanity 10.0« be introduced?

Exact times can be estimated when we have an initial understanding of the extent of acceptance. It is not clear, whether new boundary conditions, such as catastrophes will come our way. These could increase the pressure to act and speed up the introduction of »Humanity 10.0«.

The two models shown in the figure below are possible scenarios for the introduction.

Continuous introduction

Issues/trends with the greatest importance/urgency are evaluated relatively quickly

Introduction after "completion"

The Values/rating system will be "completed", then the introduction for issues/trends takes place

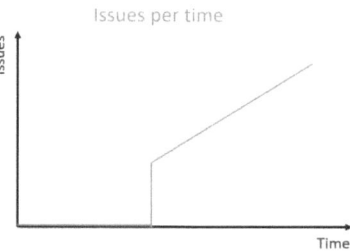

Figure 12: Scenarios for the introduction over time

It will take time before »Humanity 10.0« will reach the stage where fundamental ratings can be carried out and the insights gained can be implemented.

The "continuous introduction" is operational more quickly, since it is not dependent on a minimum number of rated issues.

»Humanity Points« are, however, not directly available as the rating of issues are only gradually aligned with each other.

If »Humanity Points« are introduced directly, it makes sense to plan more time at the beginning; depicted in the figure by "Introduction after completion". In this case, the issue ratings are already aligned to each other right from the start.

The possibility to acquire entitlements for »Humanity Points« is intended as motivation for the participation in »Humanity 10.0«. This entitlement is independent of the introduction scenario.

We humans have always pursued moral values. There are many differently well-defined "values". For instance, a set of values was already compiled with the definition of human rights.
The »Humanity 10.0« - values/rating system could serve to update this Furthermore, an additional incentive system for observance of human rights would also be available.

"Point systems" already exist for the achievement of individual goals, which also predominantly fulfil their purpose. However, the development of such a comprehensive global point system for »Humanity Points« requires a lot of time and resources.
In the context of the introduction of »Humanity 10.0«, it should be considered, exactly which global goals should be pursued and how global »Humanity Points« must be designed.
With the 5 areas of focus as the lowest common denominator, »Humanity 10.0« would be ideally suitable, particularly for the biggest global challenges. Ideally, we must try to make »Humanity 10.0« visible the world over. The ideas of »Humanity 10.0« should be spread by the people, communities, organizations worldwide and the movement of »Humanity 10.0« must network globally. It will take some time before global »Humanity 10.0« - structures are operational.

»Humanity 10.0« is not "either global or local".
The approach is always related to the issues.
There are issues that are of global, as well as of local significance.
Others have a stronger local importance, and in some cases the

global importance is predominant.

The global (for humanity as a whole and the entire environment), as well as the local importance (for the community and close surroundings) are deeply rooted in »Humanity 10.0«. In principle, global and local issues are always considered simultaneously. The primary allocation of issues can already be recognised with the first assessment.

»Humanity 10.0« can be introduced to clear local structures, such as regions, countries, and in communities by local »Humanity 10.0«-organisations, as well as to global structures such as the United Nations, corporations, and NGOs by the globally-networking »Humanity 10.0« - organisations.

Governments should desperately be looking for a mechanism such as »Humanity 10.0«, since they are currently having to cope with more and more time pressure regarding the problems of the people placing their trust in them. This does not always function without conflicts and people are not always grateful for good governance. »Humanity 10.0« would allow decision processes to take place earlier and with adequate participation by all.

The following is a short and general remark on change, or rather introduction processes.

In control engineering, transition processes from one state to a new state have been studied and described in mathematical form. The following is a brief non-control engineering explanation.

Following variants are available to regulate transition processes:

a) The I "(absolutely) want" wish dominates, reality is ignored.
    ⇒ Objective is never achieved

b) Everyone is immediately convinced and systematically
    work on the achievement of the goal
    ⇒ fastest variant, however not realistic

c) After apparent rapid success, the target level overshot the
    mark (exaggeration)
    ⇒ despite the high effort, the achievement of the objective
       is delayed because of necessary corrections

d) After a phase of persuasion, everyone works in an orderly
    manner towards achievement of the objective.
    ⇒ low-effort and fast achievement of the objective.

Even non-control engineers recognise that variant d) should be strived for.
In practise, unfortunately variant c) overshooting (exaggerating) often occurs. Sometimes less is more.

As the previous reflections show, the introduction of »Humanity 10.0« will be challenging.
But where there's is a will, there will be a way.

Part 5: Motivation

Drivers for change

There are countless studies on people's behaviour and what influences this behaviour and how. In addition to the research into fundamental contexts, the ability to influence people also plays a major role.

People are no longer only influenced via the current technological possibilities, but also systematically manipulated. Manipulations are often used to enforce special interests or when life situations or potential developments differ more and more from reality. Manipulations can possibly achieve short-term success. However, objective reality will correct manipulations in the long-run.

For example, if someone is driven to stop eating, that person will die, regardless of whether something other has been suggested to him until his dying breath.

Manipulations will continue to occur; however, we have the choice, we do not have to follow them.

In reality, the following motivations (not manipulations) are par-ticularly important, in bringing future developments into focus and getting people to participate.

Basic motivations arise for example from:

- Meeting basic material needs;
- Achieving non-material satisfaction.

Drivers for action result, for example from:

- The desire to meet basic needs and satisfaction;
- The fear that basic needs and satisfaction may not be secured.

If a life-threatening animal pursues us, we will use our intelligence to "run-away". Thus, fear is what saves us in the short-term. In the long-term, we will think about how to deal with this danger.

The solutions how to protect ourselves from danger can be that we avoid danger, get out of its way, or actively fight it. In our example we avoid the territory of the animal, we get into a safe vehicle or we will defend ourselves with weapons against the animal's attacks.

»Humanity 10.0«, as a concept for the future, focuses on "the protection from danger", securing the basic needs and long-term satisfaction of us humans and utilises the future as a ray of hope.

Although fear is a very important motivation, »Humanity 10.0« does not aim to fuel it. However, for a variety of reasons, we currently cannot suppress our fear for the future of humanity.

At this point, there is one thing we do not want to forget. All those who work for the well-being of us humans deserve our thanks and recognition!
It makes no difference at all, whether it is a matter of short-term problem-solving or medium- and long-term concepts, whether the power of persuasion or fear serve as motivation or people are won over to the cause in other ways.
Was is good per se, will stay good.

»Humanity 10.0« is intended to create a movement that unites and supports all the forces serving humans. The generated potential could lead to developments serving progress becoming common standards.

Positive effects

»Humanity 10.0« brings about many beneficial effects:

1. Reflection about issues;
2. Identifying ideas for improvements;
3. Contexts/holistic approach;
4. Rating the actual status of issues;
5. Rating of trend(s)/idea(s) related to issues;
6. Joint implementation of solution(s)
7. Linking »Humanity Points« to persons/organisations.

Which effects have the greatest significance depends on the issue and the goals set. Even if the »Humanity 10.0« - values/rating system does not lead to the quantification of the rating of the issue, questioning the issue will stimulate improvements.
However, we achieve the most improvements if we go through all the steps up to the formation of the »Humanity Points« and go on to link the »Humanity Points« to persons and organizations.
We can make use of »Humanity 10.0« for individual topics, such as the environment and climate protection. There are however many further challenges, which are partly connected to each other.

»Humanity 10.0« would be suitable for looking at the challenges in context and simultaneously managing them more efficiently.
We should not miss this opportunity!

Benefits for …

In case the benefits listed so far were not able to convince all of you yet, the next sections will look at the benefits of »Humanity 10.0« for selected persons/organisations. The benefits result from the difference between the current situation without the use of »Humanity 10.0« ideas and the future incorporating them.

The current situations have different implications for individuals and organisations. Their assessments of the situation may differ from reality, particularly if they do not look at it from a neutral, objective point of view.
Some benefits may not be immediately apparent. It is not possible to highlight the benefits for all organisations and every individual. The "groups" following their own ideas may deny any benefits stemming from »Humanity 10.0 «. All the above leads to different evaluations of the benefits.

The following are examples of the potential of »Humanity 10.0«, which result from benefits for…

… the people

»Humanity 10.0« is created for us humans. We are at the centre of the idea and the plan. All people benefit from improvements for societies.
We humans and our life situations are all very different, which is why it is impossible to list the benefits for each individual person or group of people.

»Humanity 10.0« is a new, promising, and practical initiative. For many, this is still not sufficient argument to spring into action. But surely what we all want is a bright future?

Particularly after the chaotic coronavirus pandemic, »Humanity 10.0« could serve as a vision with very concrete goals and provide hope and a new beginning for many people.

All the improvements in individual countries and big organisations have a decisive influence on the life of us humans. Therefore, mainly these will be considered.

The benefits for some groups of people will be pointed out under *"Questions and Answers"* on the following website: *www.humanity10.org*

... the UN (United Nations)

As the largest global organisation, the UN, the main aim of which is to work towards the wellbeing of all people on earth, is of central importance.

Despite the very good work in many areas, it does not live up to the role it is supposed to play, or rather it cannot fulfil its role. Resources are often lacking, in order to solve problems in the short-term because the UN is ultimately dependent on national donors. National interests therefore play a major role in many UN institutions. This dilemma is most obvious in the UN Security Council. All people have a right to peace, security, and the resolution of conflicts. In any conflict, people suffer and insecurity and desperation spread. In the UN Security Council, deadlocks seem to dominate, instead of workable solutions. The reasons for these blockades are incomprehensible to many people. This damages the reputetion of the entire UN.

The visibility of the UN is given in the case of humanitarian aid in conflicts and disasters; however, visions and long-term strategies are lacking. Concrete plans and detailed proposals for shaping the future of humanity are not readily identifiable.
This gap could be closed, or at least reduced with the help of »Humanity 10.0«.

... the EU (European Union)

The EU is the currently the most progressive confederation of states. Nowhere else are so many states with their own, sometimes varying interests so closely linked to each other. Due to some "construction errors" when it was founded, slow decision-making processes and attempts to divide the European countries, turbulences occur repeatedly.

The EU is a prime example of the necessary interaction between the individual peoples in order to be able to master future challenges.

The EU follows democratic principles. Sometimes, these are even questioned by EU members. Perhaps because democracies must be safeguarded at great expense and do not always work efficiently.

With »Humanity 10.0«, the EU would have a unifying strategic initiative to protect democracy and further develop the societies in the countries. An intelligently designed value/assessment system can lead to a direct creation of new common social standards.

... governments

Individual movements, organisations and thematically-oriented initiatives are part of a healthy democracy and do not endanger the state or society.

»Humanity 10.0« is an initiative that aims to initiate a more active discussion about the future and necessary social changes. A major advantage of this is that differences of opinion become visible at an early stage. In this way, they can be resolved before anything happens.

Strategic thinking would be the job of governments. However, these are increasingly driven by short-term governance. With the coronavirus pandemic a great deal of potential for improvement came to light. An obsessive opposition to government decisions prevails in many cases. This is not helpful, especially not during a crisis.

It would be beneficial to have important decisions and emergency plans prepared by a neutral organisation/initiative. The participation of all individuals and organisations in »Humanity 10.0« makes it possible to capture people's ideas and visions at an early stage.

»Humanity 10.0« does not aim to and cannot take over executive tasks but rather to cooperate with governments. Governments would directly benefit from a stronger sense of togetherness amongst all people, as well as early identification of solutions to upcoming challenges.

... globally operating corporations

Economy has become so globalised that any disruption in supply chains and collaboration networks has significant effects. Globally operating corporations require worldwide and reliable standards for cooperation. This refers not only to technical standards, but also social standards.

In many corporations, social standards are observed and to a certain extent, employees can profit from their success. Nevertheless, for many people, large corporations are a symbol of the change of the social market economy to a kind of "predatory capitalism". The fact that corporations "only follow market mechanisms" does not make things any better.

Corporations can play an important role in overcoming the world's challenges, especially in the area of climate protection. However, they also need to better understand and embrace their overall social remit. Some managements have already realised that appropriate changes are necessary. In those cases, it should be easier to support »Humanity 10.0« as a future-oriented idea.

... religious organisations

Religions have a long tradition in the history of humanity. Although many religions share similar values, there are significant disagreements as well as conflicts between them. Many people find it increasingly difficult to understand this disagreement and refusal to reform and are turning their backs on religion. At the same time, they find no equivalent alternative for orientation in their lives.

It should be in the religions' own interest that all people are once again more strongly connected and follow transparent humanistic values.
These are precisely the goals of »Humanity 10.0«. What should God or other holy figures have against us humans voluntarily

and steadfastly following more meaningful values, which protect the climate and the environment?

... political groupings

There are many existing parties or political groupings.

If a party or group only accepts its own ideological specifications, it will oppose everything else. Opposition purely for the sake of opposition is also counterproductive. Fortunately, most parties or groupings are capable of tolerance and cooperation and do not insist on distinctions which may seem necessary. Cooperation usually results depending on the issues at hand.

This issue-related approach is exactly what »Humanity 10.0« aims for.

»Humanity 10.0« seeks the best objective compromises. This is especially promising when opinions and objective ratings are processed "impartially" and decisions are prepared accordingly. In this way, unnecessary disputes between the individual parties can be eliminated, and finding solutions would be considerably easier.

The members of the individual parties can also better follow their conscience and always strive for the best for us humans. »Humanity 10.0« could create more continuity in governance and this, in turn, could lead to less stress during elections or changes of government.

... social organisations

Social organisations keep life going in many parts of the world. However, because of individualism, changing values and dominant social systems, their work is becoming more and more difficult. There is a lack of helpers, money and partially even of moral support.

To get involved and do good deeds is something that we humans have instilled in us from the day we are born. Although many people find it difficult to bring themselves to do that. Regardless whether it is resignation, laziness or for other reasons, additional motivation would not be amiss. Why should somebody who gets involved in society or even devoted to a cause, not get something in return?

Mutual appreciation cannot just be organised, however »Humanity Points« could help to make achievements more visible and provide additional motivation for more engagement in the community.

... non-profit / non-governmental organisations

Non-profit and non-governmental-organisations were usually established for very specific purposes and represent an important pillar in our societies. In many cases, the reason for their establishment is to solve problems in the short-term; additional medium- and long-term goals and strategies are not always in place.

The focus on a specific purpose sometimes leads to a kind of "tunnel vision". In the struggle to get members on board, other organisations may be considered as competition rather than partners.

In today's world, however, all progressive social forces need to join forces to meet the challenges faced. »Humanity 10.0« aims to serve as precisely this bond and motivate more people to engage in all types of initiatives for society.

... the media

The media scene is just as diverse as people, communities, and societies.
Radio/TV, short message services, print media, platforms for storing any kind of content use different approaches and technologies, but all of them organise the exchange of information between people.
Differences exist in terms of positioning in societies. The media can take sides or remain neutral, reality can be well or not so well portrayed.

Every day, those responsible for content ask themselves "what could people be interested in, what is important, what

should be brought out and how should it be published?"
The overall concept of »Humanity 10.0« could put a huge package of the topics that concern all people in various formats in place, over an unlimited period of time.
Bringing together the diverse issues should be just as exciting as the discussions about which priorities we humans have and what »Humanity Points« should ultimately be awarded for.

Why should the media not set positive trends?
Developing the future together and with an optimistic outlook could compensate for the umpteenth catastrophe news.

... all

One proposal of »Humanity 10.0« is that communities and groups of organisations develop their own initiatives for the future of humanity. In this way everyone can contribute and further develop, within the scope of their own possibilities and ideas, in their special fields.
For example, the programme of an initiative called "Art for Humanity" would have a different focus than that of the initiative "Science for Humanity," but both would follow the same common visions and goals. In this way, societies can effectively develop further, while sharing efforts.

With the values/rating system, »Humanity 10.0« aims to create a framework whereby individual initiatives and positive achievements of each individual person, groups of people and organisations can become more comprehensible and transparent.

»Humanity 10.0« self-correction mechanism

Problems often occur in organisations, such as:

- Goals are no longer consistently pursued;
- The organisation is preoccupied with itself;
- Necessary adjustments to new circumstances are not carried out.

To prevent these problems, »Humanity 10.0« aims to install its own mechanism.
»Humanity 10.0« is itself regularly assessed according to the values/rating system.
That means the question is posed:
"Is »Humanity 10.0« positive or negative for:

- humans,
- their close surroundings,
- their community,
- the entire environment, and
- humanity as a whole?"

This monitoring takes place transparently. In this way potential for improvement is identified and appropriate measures can be taken.

Further advantages

»Humanity 10.0« and democracy

An optimistic attitude is necessary for every vision and every goa . »Humanity 10.0« is an idea with a plan for the development of the future of humanity.
Even if »Humanity 10.0« should not immediately fall on fertile ground, »Humanity 10.0« or something of the kind will be necessary in the mid- and long-term. Otherwise, we humans will not be around for very much longer.

»Humanity 10.0« aims to provide hope.
It is however, by no means populist. Many benefits are shown, which arise, when using »Humanity 10.0«, however »Humanity 10.0« demands quite a lot from us humans. We must think, rethink and change. Everyone must take more responsibility for themselves and for the community.

»Humanity 10.0« aims to further develop democracy, as there is no alternative to democracy. Why is that?
We humans always strive for freedom and autonomy. We can achieve these in democratic societies. In a democracy, even individual dictatorial approaches are tolerated. A dictatorship, on the other hand, will always fight democratic developments for fear of losing its own power. Nevertheless, there is no dictatorship which really remained in power for long.

We all need to develop our democracies further, today, more than ever!

Create more "values"

Money and material values are unequally distributed. Those who have money do not necessarily want to share it with anyone.
To some extent, there is a willingness to be charitable.
Those with little money need or want more. Obtaining money illegally is not in the social interest.

The »Humanity 10.0« - »Humanity Points« would lead to those values that are immediately important for us humans to play a greater role. These values would initially not be connected to money or other material values. They are aligned solely to the issues and their meaning for us humans.
In principle, we humans know the values that are important to us. However, in many societies, these do not yet have the appropriate significance.

With »Humanity 10.0«, somebody who has little money could suddenly gain "values" and satisfaction without taking anything away from anyone else.
There are no limits to the ideas for the application of »Humanity 10.0« and the way of using »Humanity Points«. Some ideas are described in this book.

The right measure

People are occasionally too greedy. In most cases, this has negative effects. It makes no difference, what the strong desire behind this greed is aimed at. It is not a good thing to be too greedy with respect to consumption and to consume more and more.
Overdoing it when limiting consumption, particularly in the form of bans, can be counterproductive.

Let us look at an example from the area of environmental protection. Air travel and cruises have a poor environmental record. Nevertheless, banning them would not lead to social acceptance. Is this because people are unreasonable? It is more the fact that the step from the current status to total sacrifice, is simply too big for some people. Everyone knows very well how difficult it is to change; intelligent approaches are called for.

What would happen if all those who had clearly achieved a certain level of environmental protection, for example 50 tons of CO_2 savings, were to receive, in return, say 10 tons of CO_2 air travel and cruises as an "exclusive service" from society?
Translated into the approach of »Humanity 10.0«, this means

that everyone can get something back from the service performed. All those totally in favour of environmental protection would still not have to take flights or go on cruises. But maybe there is something else a person would like for which »Humanity Points« could be used.

We will achieve the best effect if many people are encouraged to participate. The "heroic deeds" of some will be difficult to achieve for many. "Heroic deeds" are nevertheless extremely important as shining examples. Expecting dedicated "heroes" to be perfect and do everything right is not fitting. It is hard enough to upkeep belief in positive change and actively contribute towards it.

Strengthening social norms

In all societies, it is necessary to encourage achievement and the necessary commitment for the good of all. Unfortunately, this achievement principle does not always work. In some cases, rewards are given for non-achievement or poor achievement. This sends a negative signal to all people and reduces motivation. Incidentally, these unjust rewards occur in all walks of life.

But much more dramatic are situations in which moral boundaries are deliberately crossed for personal gain. Although the situations in question are perfectly clear to everyone, no sanctions can be imposed, for example because of legal loopholes or the (often emotional) damage caused is underestimated.
Such examples are a slap in the face for all righteous people. Even more - people expect clear sanctions in such situations and are disappointed. This has a long-term negative impact on the development of society.

In the context of the rating using by the »Humanity 10.0« - values/rating system, the values can be newly classified by us humans, for example, as being particularly important. Since many »Humanity Points« are awarded for the issues with these values, the values are continuously promoted.
There is nothing to be said against the introduction of sanctions

such as the withdrawal of acquired »Humanity Points«, if important values are violated or serious damage is done.
This would allow for new rating standards. Gaps in the legal systems could even be closed.

More freedom through transparency

»Humanity 10.0« is intended to stimulate innovative thinking about existing issues.

It is currently feared that freedom could be restricted by transparency. If we take a closer look at the contexts, the fears stem primarily from the fact that transparency is or could be abused.

Existing legal systems are adapting far too late, especially to technological developments and the abuse that usually accompanies them. This can be seen very clearly, for example, in the way that personal data is currently handled or the spreading of untruths on the Internet. Even on a global scale, technologies are being misused faster than possible negative consequences are being considered.

With the »Humanity 10.0« - values/rating system, potential abuse would become apparent sooner.
Each time a technology is rated, the negative effects for us humans and the environment would be questioned. This would make it possible to promptly initiate changes in the law or, if necessary, sanctions.

If existing rules and appropriate sanctions are truly transparent to everyone, this would act as a deterrent and stop one or the other from breaking the rules.
We humans "must" find ways to let off steam, sometimes we want to be reckless. If we apply the criteria of »Humanity 10.0«, there would be nothing to prevent us from creating newfound freedom through more clarity.

We already looked at the example of allowing people to drive "too fast" on approved race tracks. It would be clear to everyone on the racetrack that they could come to harm even through no

fault of their own. Those who want to drive on the racetrack must protect themselves in such a way that the general public does not have to step in to cover for any damage that may occur.
Since this provides additional freedom, it would be even more justified to sanction speeding on public roads.
Quite simple really - isn't it?

CO_2

In the case of »Humanity 10.0«, the protection of close surroundings and entire environment are included as rating criteria for every issue. This consistent approach means that there is a good chance of being better able to enforce environmental protection.

In principle, it would be fair if every person could produce the same amount of CO_2 or other "pollution" and, in return, would receive annual "pollution certificates". This approach would, almost certainly provoke, many opinions with thousands of reasons against its feasibility. There are already some, albeit still tentative, attempts in this direction.

With the issuance and trading of "CO_2 certificates", the first steps have already been taken for the organisations.
A weak point here is that money plays the decisive role. That is, whoever has money or earns enough money through business can pollute without major consequences.
Even if the "CO_2 certificates" come at a high price, that would not change the situation. In many cases, the costs are passed on to us humans and we are then talked into believing that the issuance of the "CO_2 certificates" is responsible for this.
Through the current policy of "cheap money (almost no interest on loans)", loans for securing business are cheap. Is this not a way of conveniently co-financing "CO_2 certificates", and therefore pollution?

Optimisation regarding one area of focus, such as CO_2 production often leads to new challenges in other areas. That is why an overall strategy like »Humanity 10.0« would be so important.

Proceeding in the same way?

Let us go back to the beginning of the book, to the "Wake up!" survey.

The numerous and sometimes confusing challenges certainly leave us with an uneasy feeling for the future.

We must tackle the challenges together.

Perhaps even children can become role models for their parents.

However, we need everyone, young – old, poor – rich, ...

The necessary changes will be impossible to manage without new ideas. Since good advice is needed for good ideas, everyone should really participate.

»Humanity 10.0« and its benefits is an idea, a concept, and a plan, already on the table – open for discussion and improvement.

Part 6: Finally

Summary

Humanity faces a myriad of challenges.
Although many people continue to deny it, these challenges are gradually becoming very real and many perceive them as being impossible to overcome.

»Humanity 10.0« aims to tackle precisely this task.

Our world has already become incredibly complex and unmanageable and is likely to get worse. The relevant challenges affect every human being and encroach on all areas of life.

Many individual and sound initiatives already exist, however, these do not, unfortunately, add up to a whole.

Humans are by no means perfect, but they have survived so far because of their adaptability.

»Humanity 10.0« relies on simple approaches and well-known mechanisms, in order to reach out to all people.

The goals of »Humanity 10.0« are:

- To ensure the survival of the human race;
- To further develop society(s); and
- To increase people's sense of well-being.

The goals indicate that this is about a broad, integrative approach for the future. The focus should no longer be on the current and sometimes over-emphasised differences between people.
All people form one community, which is the key to overcoming the challenges faced.

We humans need hope and motivation for the future, for example in the form of visions. The visions and goals of »Humanity 10.0« should appeal to all people and give them courage.

Implementing these goals will be made easier if the following requirements are fulfilled:

- Reality is not questioned;
- A stronger focus is placed on the future;
- The past "only" serves as a source of experience;
- The community becomes more important;
- We humans use the concept of "thinking in the original position".

»Humanity 10.0« wants to achieve a unifying effect on a simple common basis. This basis is the »Humanity 10.0« - values/rating system. It defines the areas of focus that are relevant for all the goals, issues, trends, and ideas.

The assessment/rating is done by means of 5 simple questions. Is the issue or trend good or bad for:

- Humanity as a whole?
- My/our community?
- The individual human (you/me)?
- My/our close surroundings?
- The entire environment?

New insights already emerge after first qualitative ratings using the values/rating system. These can directly influence priorities for our actions.

It is just as important for the rating of issues and trends, how good or bad these are in detail. The quantitative ratings help to make this become transparent and comparable. The results are objectively rated issues and trends. With the help of these ratings based on reality, priorities can be further optimised.

»Humanity Points« are created after coordinating the ratings, issues, and trends. These have an instant value due to the positive aspects for humanity, the community, the people and the local and the entire environments.

Issues and trends are often linked to persons and organisations. Further benefits arise as a result of this link. Individuals and organizations can be motivated towards the areas of focus that are important for us humans.

Since »Humanity Points« have a value, they can be used as a kind of alternative "currency".
Albeit "possibilities for exchange" must be created.
»Humanity Points« could be exchanged for …
– there are no limits to the ideas.

It is now clear what should evolve from »Humanity 10.0«.
How can it be implemented?

Some keys to success are:

- A convincing concept;
- »Humanity 10.0« develops parallel to the prevailing circumstances and other ideas;
- Simple and familiar things are made use of;
- An extensive participation of all people is possible;
- »Humanity 10.0« is open and flexible;
- The solution-finding is based on issues;
- »Humanity 10.0« can be used both globally and locally.

Examples for the use of simple and familiar things are the awareness of point systems and currency, use of existing tools and aids, and that our characteristics will be considered objectively.
A new platform will be created for »Humanity 10.0«, which uses established technologies.

The idea should be established in people's minds by impulses and a »Humanity 10.0« "brand" should facilitate its recognition.

History and individual sensitivities often prevent solutions being found and therefore play a secondary role in the context of »Humanity 10.0«. All the persons and organisations involved in finding a solution are not assaulted by »Humanity 10.0«, but rather incorporated in a neutral, relevant, and solution-oriented manner.

Everyone should cooperate in the further development, as well as in the implementation of »Humanity 10.0«.

The necessary motivation for change arises from the transparent depiction of what is important for us humans. The existing social structures will be used for implementation.

»Humanity 10.0« relies on us humans.

There will be changes. Each one of us will be affected. No country will be spared. Future challenges can only be overcome together. We no longer have time for people to concentrate on solely pursuing their own goals!

»Humanity 10.0« calls for an evolution with the help of well thought through and sustainable changes.

If we do not initiate the necessary changes immediately, we humans are facing very turbulent times or certain doom.

Dear reader

Yes – »Humanity 10.0« is utopian.
As utopian, as people flying into space or millions of books being stored on a small chip or cars that drive on their own or robots which act independently.

»Humanity 10.0« is perhaps not new at all? Where and when have you encountered something similar? Any hint would be appreciated and it is important that all those thinking similarly come together. Please forward any information you may have to info@humanity10.org.

»Humanity 10.0« is (currently) not feasible - ???
This has always been the way; whatever has been created by humans was also changed by humans.
Most adjustments were considered beforehand, often unimaginable reactions to changes which happened and were sooner or later inevitable.

»Humanity 10.0« is not fully developed – that is how it is.
Everything needs to develop. Fruits must ripen before they can be eaten with appetite.
However, every development / every ripening needs a beginning.

...

This is the first, almost certainly not perfect book, written by an ordinary human being.
One thing remains, despite all the possible criticism.

There is somebody out there who is standing up for you.
Is that not what you have always wanted?

See you soon

If you have read this book carefully, you can guess what will happen next with »Humanity 10.0«.

A next step is to specifically approach people and organisations to get them involved in the future of humanity. Engaging in conversation is a very important step. It will be interesting to see how people respond.

Anybody in doubt as to how he or she can practically contribute to »Humanity 10.0«
can visit the website *www.humanity10.org*
or contact *info@humanity10.org*.

We need a lot of supporters and active collaborators for »Humanity 10.0«.

Let's do this!

We look forward to meeting you.

Appendix

Appendix 1
Detailed description of the values/rating system

In the chapter "The values/rating system" in Part 2, the basic procedure was already described. Reading this part again could clarfy the following explanations.

In this appendix, a proposal for the structure of a flexible values/rating for issues / trends is presented. First factors for the prioritisation of the individual ratings and important aspects for their selection are addressed.
The more thorough the application of the rating system, the more iteration loops for balancing the factors are likely to be necessary. At the end of the detailed rating, »Humanity Points« are allocated per issue/trend.

An exact quantification for the establishment of »Humanity Points« is indispensable. Many aspects and influencing variables must be considered for the quantification. Therefore scientists, politicians, workers, and employees, in other words all people are asked to cooperate at this stage.

The explanations in this section are not yet very comprehensive. They are intended to indicate the direction and to illustrate the first ideas for a quantification.

The following rating steps, ratings and rating factors are proposed and looked at in more detail in the next sections:

1   Assessment of the issue

    ⇒ Points per issue and area of focus

2.   Importance of issue per area of focus

    ⇒ Factor per issue and area of focus

3.   Assessment trend for issue

    ⇒ Points per issue and area of focus

4. Importance trend for issue
   ⇒ Factor per issue and area of focus
5. Importance of the areas of focus
   ⇒ Factors for the areas of focus
6. Rating points per issue
   ⇒ Points achieved for the issue
7. Adjustment of the rating points
   ⇒ Additional factors for scaling

Re. 1. Assessment of the issue

This first step is relatively simple.
Rating ranges and steps must be defined. These must be suitable in order to be able to represent a good rating of the current status for the considered issue.
An example would be school grades with a rating range from grade 1 to grade 6 and a step size of one.

For some areas of focus, it may not be possible to make useful ratings. In these cases, a "neutral rating" is introduced and this area of focus for the rating is omitted.
The result is a rating system with steps in both positive and negative directions.
The following figure shows a "neutral rating". The rated issue has no connection to the area of focus "entire environment". Ratings are carried out for all the areas of focus in the determined breakdown of steps, that is 3 steps in the positive and 3 steps in the negative direction.

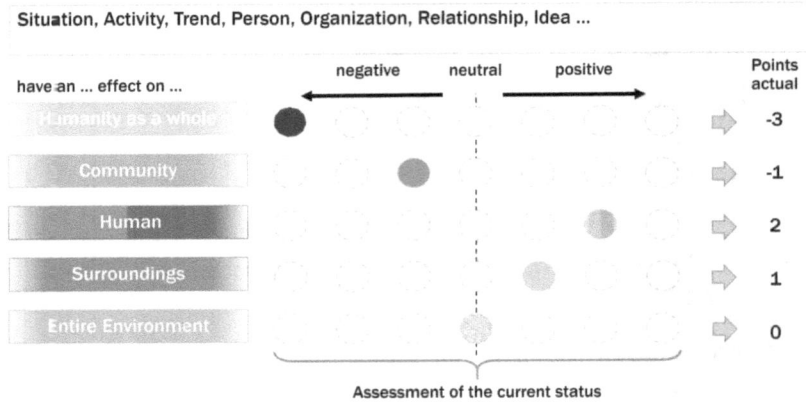

Figure 13: Rating of the current status of an issue

This current rating for the issue is a first step, it does not, however reveal anything about its importance.

Re. 2. The importance of issues per area of focus

In many cases, the importance of an issue differs for the five areas of focus, "humanity as a whole", "community", "humans", "close surroundings", and "entire environment".
Regardless of the ratings in step 1, the importance of an issue for the areas of focus is determined in step 2. The greater the importance, the greater the rating factor.

In our example, see the figure "Importance of issues per area of focus", five rating steps with a step size of one were introduced. This results in rating factors (weighting matter) from 1 to 5. In this example, the importance of the area of focus, "humanity as a whole" is the greatest.

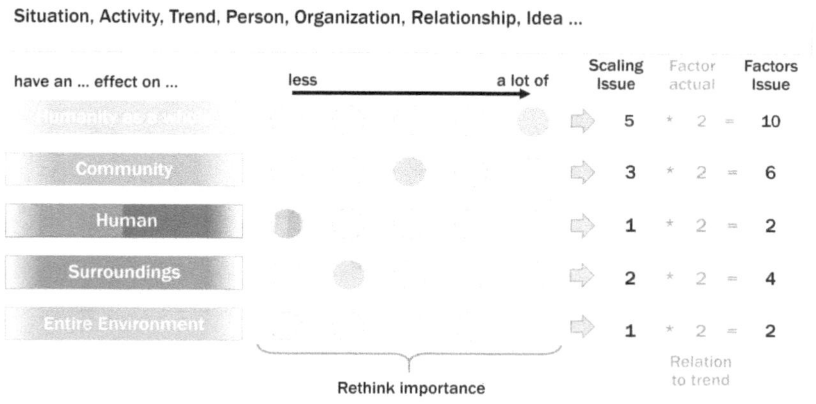

Situation, Activity, Trend, Person, Organization, Relationship, Idea ...

have an ... effect on ...	less — a lot of	Scaling Issue	Factor actual		Factors Issue
Humanity as a whole		5	* 2	=	10
Community		3	* 2	=	6
Human		1	* 2	=	2
Surroundings		2	* 2	=	4
Entire Environment		1	* 2	=	2

Rethink importance

Relation to trend

Figure 14: Importance of issues per area of focus

The figure shows a further factor (factor current).

This factor can be introduced in order to determine, which assessments are of greatest importance; those for the current situation or those for the future.

So, there is another factor (factor trend). This is included in the calculation when assessing the importance of the trend to the issue in step 4.

In our example, the ratings of the current situation are twice as important as those for the trends, therefore the "factor current" =2 and the "factor trend" = 1.

The factors for the importance of the issue per area of focus result from:

*Factors matter = weighting matter * factor current*

After the importance is clarified, the quantitative rating of the current situation for the issue can take place.

The assessment of the issue for each of the areas of focus results in:

Points current (step 1) * factors matter (step 2)
   = current points per area of focus.

Sum of current points per area of focus
   = points for the current status of the issue.

Re. 3. Assessment of trend per issue

Future developments can be estimated for many issues. These trends can be more important than the rating of the issue.

Initially, the times are established for which an assessment of the development of the issue is to be made.
In our example, medium-term (e.g. after 5 years) and long-term (e.g. after 10 years) forecasts are planned for the development of the issue.
As far as possible, a rating for both points in time is aimed at.

If predictions are not possible, a "neutral" assessment is made. The ratings are set equal to zero and no points are included in the overall rating.

The following figure, "assessing trends" is about the assessment of trends in connection with the area of focus "human". The rating at the time "time2 (long-term)" is a "neutral rating". In addition, the subject matter has no significance for the entire environment, even in the future.
There are "neutral ratings" for both time1 and time2.

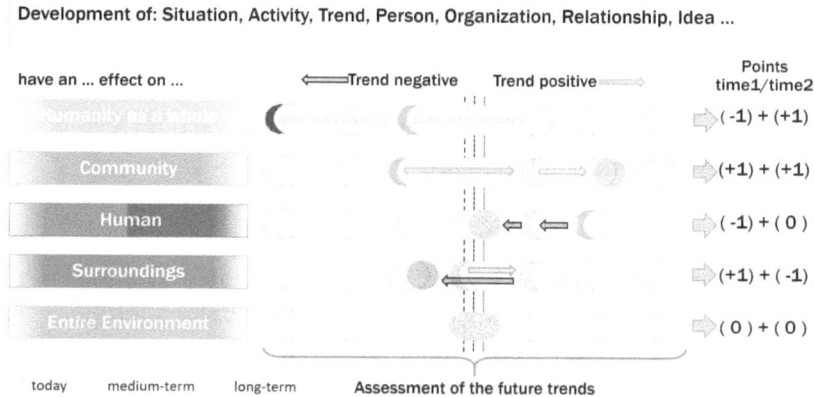

Development of: Situation, Activity, Trend, Person, Organization, Relationship, Idea ...

Figure 15: Assessing trends

The rating times, time1 and time2 should be chosen in such a way that developments can actually take place.

For logical reasons, the entire rating should be updated, at the latest when time1 is reached. In this way progress can be monitored and a reassessment is triggered; a dynamic rating system results with a reassessment every x number of years. A regular reassessment every x number of years also allows for an adjustment of the rating standards.

In this way the ratings can be continuously improved.

Re. 4. Importance of trends for issues

Trends can be more important than the current rating of the issue. This would be adjusted, as already mentioned in step 2, by the ratio "factor current" to "factor trend".

The procedure for setting the importance of the trends for each area of focus does not differ from the procedure described in step2. The example presented in step2 is the "factor current" = 2 and the "factor trend" = 1, meaning that the rating of the current situation is more important.

If trends are to be rated higher than the current situation, the "factor trend" must be > than "factor current".

If it makes sense to evaluate the mid-term assessment differently than the long-term one, two different factors could be also used instead of one "factor trend".
For time1 (mid-term), the factor trend1 would be set and for time2 (long-term) the factor trend2 would be set.

In principle, it would even be possible to vary the factors for the importance of the point in time (current, mid-term or long-term) again per area of focus. However, this makes the rating more complicated and there must be comprehensible reasons for the choice of factors.

There are three separate ratings after the rating of the trends, these vary in importance, one current rating, one for time1 and one for time2. After merging the results, the rating of the issue would be complete.

Further factors will be suggested in the following steps.

Re. 5. Importance of the areas of focus

So far, the importance of the areas of focus for the current ratings of issues and their trends was only rated using the factors described. This is, so to speak, the default state.

However exceptional situations, for example catastrophes, can occur. Such exceptional situations require exceptional measures and a change in the areas of focus.
Thus, for example, during the coronavirus pandemic, the community and humanity as a whole became more important than the welfare of the individual (person).
In these exceptional situations, it would be good if the values/rating system could continue to be used so that issues would not need to be newly rated fundamentally.

Therefore, a further factor is proposed for the values/rating system, that enables the re-evaluation of the areas of focus.
The areas of focus no longer have the basic factor1, but they

are allocated a factor, which has been adapted to the situation. In this way, the previously valid ratings can continue to be used in exceptional situations and still be adapted to the specific needs of the situation.

These factors for rating the areas of focus, that are tailored to the specific needs of the situation, could also be used to vary social models. A society with a strong individualisation could thus increase the importance of the area of focus "human". The areas of focus "community" and "humanity as a whole" would be rated higher by societies oriented towards the common good.
The basic importance of the issues remains just as valid as the objective ratings.

Situational factors can be introduced for the rating of the current state, as well as for the mid- and long-term trends.

Re. 6. Rating per issue

Rating points for the issue result after the different ratings have been carried out.

The basic rating of the issue consists of:

Current ratings of the issue per area of focus result from

ratings of the current status of the issue (points)
multiplied by
the factor for importance issue per area of focus
multiplied by
the factor for rating difference "current/trend".

Rating of the mid-term trend of the issue result from

ratings mid-term trend issue (points)
multiplied by
the factor for importance issue per area of focus
multiplied by
the factor for rating difference "trend/current".

<u>Rating of the long-term trend</u> of the issue results from

Ratings of the long-term trend issue (points)
  multiplied by

the factor importance issue per area of focus
  multiplied by

the factor for rating difference "trend/current".

The basic rating of the issue is thereby completed.

As described under 5. "importance of issues", the areas of focus could still be estimated differently.

Since many different issues will be rated and simultaneously, proportionalities between the different issues must be maintained, a further factor will be introduced in the next section.

Re. 7. Adjustment of the rating points

The rated issues hold varying degrees of importance for society. A »Humanity Point« should, however, have a universally valid value. Therefore, a kind of standardisation is necessary. In the values/rating system, various individual ratings of issues are coordinated with each other by use of further factors. This can only be done after many individual ratings of different issues have been carried out.

The adjustments should be made possible by introducing scaling factors for the rating of the issue per area of focus. The following figure "Quantitative rating" is intended to illustrate how the calculation of the rating points is compiled using different factors.

Situation, Activity, Trend, Person, Organization, Relationship, Idea ...

Detailed ratings	Actual figure * factor	Trend figure * factor	Basis or special factor	Points issue	If needed scaling
Humanity as a whole	(-3 * 10 = -30) +	(0 * 3 = 0) =	(-30 * 1 = -30)	-30	x * -30
Community	(-1 * 6 = -6) +	(2 * 2 = 4) =	(-2 * 1 = -2)	-2	x * -2
Human	(2 * 2 = 4) +	(1 * 1 = 1) =	(5 * 1 = 5)	5	x * 5
Surroundings	(1 * 4 = 4) +	(0 * 4 = 0) =	(4 * 1 = 4)	4	x * 4
Entire Environment	(0 * 2 = 0) +	(0 * 2 = 0) =	(0 * 1 = 0)	0	x * 0
				-23	xxx

Figure 16: Quantitative rating

In the figure, one issue that is decisive for "humanity as a whole" is currently so negative that other areas of focus cannot compensate for it.

The person that this issue is assigned to receives negative »Humanity Points«.

Consequently, this issue would have to be seriously improved mid-term in the interests of "humanity as a whole".

Further factors are thinkable, for example, in the transitional period, when a new issue is incorporated into the values/rating system.

As already mentioned, the above should only illustrate a possible approach.

The development of the »Humanity Points« will still require extensive iteration steps.

A checklist for the described rating approach is available in electronic form at *www.humanity10.org*.

List of figures

Zeitfracht Medien GmbH
Ferdinand-Jühlke-Straße 7
99095 Erfurt, Deutschland
produktsicherheit@kolibri360.de